Jesus is worth your wait!
Psalm 130:5
♡ Amy Rauman

D1501259

WHEN YOUR
WAIT
BECOMES YOUR
WEIGHT

*Persevering When You're
Desperate for Answers
from God*

AMY RAUMAN

WESTBOW
PRESS®
A DIVISION OF THOMAS NELSON
& ZONDERVAN

NIV: Scriptures taken from the Holy Bible, New International Version®, NIV®. Copyright
© 1973, 1978, 1984, 2011 by Biblica, Inc.™ Used by permission of Zondervan. All rights
reserved worldwide. www.zondervan.com The "NIV" and "New International Version" are
trademarks registered in the United States Patent and Trademark Office by Biblica, Inc.

WestBow Press books may be ordered through booksellers or by contacting:

WestBow Press
A Division of Thomas Nelson & Zondervan
1663 Liberty Drive
Bloomington, IN 47403
www.westbowpress.com
1 (866) 928-1240

ISBN: 978-1-9736-2010-5 (sc)
ISBN: 978-1-9736-2011-2 (hc)
ISBN: 978-1-9736-2050-1 (e)

Library of Congress Control Number: 2018902072

Print information available on the last page.

WestBow Press rev. date: 04/27/2018

ACKNOWLEDGEMENTS

I'M THANKFUL TO GOD, MY Creator, as He is the One who gave me this writing assignment. I'm most grateful for the way He has grown me spiritually through this process. I'm thankful to Jesus. He is my Savior, my Redeemer and my Friend. I have an eternal hope and future because of His precious blood shed on the cross for my sins. I'm also thankful to the Holy Spirit who has inspired, taught and encouraged me through the Scriptures He has woven together in my heart and onto the pages of this book. I stand in awe at the work of the Lord and am humbled to be His child.

Thank you, Alisa, for being my dear faithful friend. You were with me the very day God gave me the assignment to write this book, and you've been on the journey with me ever since. You've encouraged me, prayed for me, celebrated with me and even challenged me at just the right times. You've reminded me to never lose sight of my first love, Jesus Christ. You've also reminded me to always complete the work that the Lord gives me, no matter who else may ever see it or know about it. I treasure your friendship.

Thank you, Bonnie. You are my sweet sister-in-Christ. Though nearly 1,800 miles have distanced us for many years, our friendship has only grown stronger over time. You have prayed for me, encouraged me and held me accountable when needed. We've shared a variety of joys, trials and sorrows together. I'm grateful that our conversations have always revolved around the Lord. Your friendship is a gift.

Thank you to my faithful and loving husband, John, and to my amazing kids, Tate and Emma. You have been my quiet supporters along the way. You never asked what I was doing day or night as I sat typing away at the computer. You just let me do my thing. I've so appreciated that. You all bring joy to my heart in ways you'll never know.

Thank you to Cynthia and the G.R.E.G. Foundation, Inc. Your Christian love and support over the years has been a blessing. You've watched me grow from a young girl to a grown adult. We've shared a variety of opportunities together including work, travel, ministry and even our passion for writing. Thank you for encouraging me and celebrating the work God has done in my life. I'm so appreciative.

Thank you to my dear Mom and Dad. You're not only my parents, you're also my friends. What a gift that is from the Lord. You've believed in me since I was a little girl and have seen God's hand at work in my life in ways I couldn't see for myself. You've loved me at my best and loved me at my worst. You've invested in both my personal and spiritual lives. You've prayed for me diligently over the years and have encouraged me with God's Word. It's been a blessing to have served and grown together in the Lord with you over the years. You've taught me to persevere and have reminded me to do everything to glorify the Name of the Lord. I'm most grateful for your unconditional love and support.

"For from him and through him and to him are all things. To him be the glory forever. Amen."

Romans 11:36

CONTENTS

PREFACE

OVER THE PAST FEW YEARS, I've hesitated sharing with many people that I started writing a book. I was fearful of what people might think of me because I've never done this type of thing before. Besides, who do I think I am anyway to write something others will find worth reading?

I've been afraid of rejection. I've been afraid of criticism. I've been afraid of making mistakes. I've also been afraid of not having the answers to the many questions that would naturally come my way when people found out the journey I was on. "How long will the book be? Who is going to publish it? When will it be done? What are you going to do with it when it's done?" And the biggest question of all, "Are you done yet?"

To be honest, I wasn't even sure if this work would be a book or Bible study until I got much farther into it. I simply saw it as an assignment from the Lord and I wanted to be faithful in completing the work so I could simply give it back to the Lord to let Him do with it as He pleases.

Over time, I've realized that it might not necessarily be the content of this book that may be the most encouraging to others. The content might not matter at all. It might simply be the fact that God was willing to use me, an ordinary Christian woman, to take an actual step of faith with God so that others could be encouraged to do the same.

As I've written this book, I've prayed for each reader to have a heart that truly desires to follow God, no matter how ridiculous or crazy His request may seem. I pray that you fear and revere God enough to say "Yes" to His calling. May you not be consumed or swayed by anyone else's opinions. This is your walk with God. Don't let anyone or anything get in your way of obeying the Lord.

I pray that men and women alike are passionate enough to walk with God that they will make adjustments to their lives in order to pursue the assignments and work God is calling them to do. I'm a woman who has seen the proof that God alone is faithful... *"The one who calls you is faithful and he will do it"* (1 Thessalonians 5:24). But I've needed to be willing to join in on the journey He's called me to without hesitation, because hesitation gives Satan a foothold, and I couldn't afford to doubt the calling God laid upon my heart. I've wanted to stand on solid ground and let God make my steps firm. I've wanted others to experience the same joy and peace that results from trusting in Him alone.

Be confident in the Lord, dear friends, wherever He is leading you. Take a step of faith and watch Him do a mighty work through you. Be an ordinary individual who is willing to walk with an extraordinary God. Enjoy the journey. Keep your eyes fixed on Him and don't look back. Be watchful and anticipate that God will faithfully do His work through you. There's nothing like experiencing God, so press on!

SUGGESTIONS FOR
USING THIS STUDY

WHEN YOUR WAIT BECOMES YOUR WEIGHT is applicable for personal or group study. It is intended for individuals of all ages and is applicable from the youngest believer in Christ to the oldest.

The questions at the end of each chapter are intended to help you grow deeper in your relationship with Jesus Christ. I encourage you to take time to really think about each question before answering it. Allow the words and Scriptures from each chapter to resonate in your heart as you ponder where God has you in life right now.

Answer the questions honestly. Sometimes that's the hardest part. Remember, this is between you and God. There's not necessarily a right or wrong answer to the questions. Most of the questions are simply designed for you to identify where you're at in your personal and spiritual life at this particular moment in time. If you prefer not to write your answers in the book, do your best to let God write the answers on your heart and mind. He wants to grow you and transform you through His Word and through this study. He wants you to become more like Him. What a privilege. Don't hold back. Immerse yourself and grow deep with God. There's nothing like experiencing Him to the full.

I'm praying for you as you walk through the pages ahead. Be encouraged. God will meet you right where you are and He will walk with you every step of the way. You are not alone.

Author's Note: For the purpose of consistency throughout this book, I've used the 1984 NIV Bible for each Scripture referenced. If you choose to look up one of the Scripture references using another version of the Bible, please be aware that the wording may be different.

1

WHAT ARE WE WAITING FOR?

CONSIDER THIS THOUGHT FOR A moment, "What do you spend the majority of your time doing while you live on this earth?" This answer could vary greatly based on the age, gender and multiple other demographics of the audience being asked. If a baby could speak, his or her answer would most likely be sleeping. For a child it may be playing. For a teen it may be studying, hanging with friends or spending time using social media. For an adult it may be working. For a retiree it may be traveling. Other time consumers for different age groups may include watching TV, using the computer, going to appointments, participating in sports and hobbies, texting, reading, driving, eating and even breathing.

But what about the idea of waiting? Have you ever given a single thought towards the idea of how much time the average person spends waiting during their life here on earth? We have all been born into a world where the motto could simply be, "Hurry Up and Wait." Not a single person is exempt from this concept. We spend far more time waiting than we'd ever guess.

Here's a list of several examples we may find ourselves waiting for, or waiting to do during our lifetime. Which ones can you relate to? Some of these are short-term waits and others require a lot of time. Some waits can be enjoyable and some can be painful. Some are funny and some are frustrating. Check the boxes next to the ones you have either experienced in the past, or are experiencing now.

- ☐ Wait for stop lights to turn green
- ☐ Wait for an injury or sickness to heal
- ☐ Wait to find out test results
- ☐ Wait for the microwave to heat up your food
- ☐ Wait for a special event to take place
- ☐ Wait to be seated or served at a restaurant
- ☐ Wait for payday to come around
- ☐ Wait to receive a response from someone
- ☐ Wait to be called on to provide an answer to a question
- ☐ Wait for a storm to pass
- ☐ Wait for someone to pick you up and give you a ride somewhere
- ☐ Wait for your turn in line (at an amusement park, the grocery store, etc.)
- ☐ Wait to use the restroom
- ☐ Wait for a movie or program to start
- ☐ Wait for hot water to come out of a faucet or shower
- ☐ Wait for commercials to end so you can watch your favorite TV program
- ☐ Wait to give or receive a gift
- ☐ Wait for seasons to change
- ☐ Wait to figure something out
- ☐ Wait for your alarm to go off in the morning
- ☐ Wait to fall asleep at night
- ☐ Wait for someone to pick up the phone when you make a call
- ☐ Wait to be asked out on a date
- ☐ Wait to be accepted into a school or university

- [ ] Wait for a traffic jam to start moving again
- [ ] Wait to be called on for an appointment from the waiting room
- [ ] Wait to receive a transplant (liver, kidney, heart, etc.)
- [ ] Wait for someone special to visit you
- [ ] Wait to go on vacation
- [ ] Wait to grow up or to turn significant ages (i.e. to vote, to drive, to live independently, etc.)
- [ ] Wait to get married
- [ ] Wait to have a baby
- [ ] Wait for an adoption process to go through
- [ ] Wait for your home to sell
- [ ] Wait for a loan to go through
- [ ] Wait to become grandparents
- [ ] Wait to retire
- [ ] Wait to be told you are loved
- [ ] Wait for difficult situations to pass
- [ ] Wait for a "big break" in life (i.e. job promotion, advancement, success)
- [ ] Wait for an apology, forgiveness, or restoration
- [ ] Wait for a jury verdict
- [ ] Wait for an appropriate time to ask a favor of someone
- [ ] Wait to accuse or ridicule someone who hurt you
- [ ] Wait for your body to reveal that your diet and exercise program is, or isn't, working
- [ ] Wait for someone to "cut to the chase" when they tell a story
- [ ] Wait to feel safe or comforted

☐ Wait to get direction from God

☐ Wait to die

☐ Other: _____

While this is certainly not an exhaustive list of the things we wait for, it offers a starting point in helping us acknowledge that we wait for a lot of different things in life. Did you check off more boxes than you expected? When I did this myself, I was surprised by the results. Waiting is a much bigger part of our lives than most of us would probably ever guess.

According to two online reference sites, www.reference.com and www.thefactsite.com, here are some interesting statistics regarding the average times people spend waiting for various things during their lifetime:

- The average person spends five years waiting in lines and queues. Roughly six months of that is waiting at traffic lights. (No wonder so many people speed up for yellow lights!)

- Americans wait an average of 20 minutes a day for the bus or train, 32 minutes whenever they visit a doctor, and 28 minutes waiting in security lines whenever they travel.

- Americans wait 21 minutes for a significant other to get ready to go out.

- Other than waiting in line, the average person spends about 43 days on hold with automated customer service. (Imagine how many times you've heard the line, "We apologize for the delay. We are experiencing a higher call volume than usual. Please continue to hold for the next available agent." Sound familiar?)

Based upon this information alone, we can see that a lot of time can be wasted if we aren't conscientious and purposeful with our periods of wait. We need to be cautious not to let our wait times become wasted times. We need to be wise in what we decide to do while we wait. Sure, sometimes our waiting periods are only a few minutes or seconds, and there's not much we can do productively to fill that time. However, what about when our wait times last days, weeks, or even years?

Realizing that waiting is a large part of everyone's life, we need to identify biblical ways that direct us on what we should do when our *wait* becomes a *weight*. Short waits can be relatively easy to endure, but when our waiting times get extended, they can quickly become a burden. The chapters ahead will address how we can best deal with the burdensome waits of life.

Extended wait times are unavoidable in this world and, as Christians, we need to learn how to handle them in a godly way. But before jumping ahead, let's think through a few questions.

DISCUSSION QUESTIONS:

1. In your personal opinion, why do you believe waiting is important?

   _____

   _____

   _____

   _____

2. What can be learned by waiting?

   _____

   _____

   _____

   _____

3. Based upon the season of life you're currently in, what areas do you find yourself waiting for the most right now?

   _____

   _____

   _____

   _____

4. Are you typically encouraged, or discouraged, while you wait? Why?

   _____

   _____

   _____

   _____

5. What is the longest you've had to wait for something? What was that experience like?

   _____

   _____

   _____

   _____

LONG FOR GOD

GENESIS 16 INTRODUCES US TO the story of Sarai and Hagar. Just like many women in the world today, Sarai longed for a child. To her disappointment, the Lord had kept her from having children, and time was not on her side. As the story unfolds we learn that Sarai was about 75 years old and her husband, Abram, was about 85 years old. I think we'd all agree that 75 years is a long time for any woman to wait for a child.

Though Sarai may have wanted children to fulfill her personal desires, we must remember what the culture was like during her time. The idea of a woman not bearing children was typically shamed by one's peers. How humiliating. The struggle of feeling like a failure would be great. The fact of becoming an outcast within her own community would have been a tremendous weight to bear. Seventy-five years of waiting for a child must have seemed overwhelming. Sarai became desperate in her hopeless state.

As a result of her personal desires not being met, Sarai chose to take the situation into her own hands. The wait became too great for her to bear so she conjured up a way to get the results she so desperately longed for. As we'll soon learn from Sarai's example, things don't work out so well when we rush or interrupt God's plans for us. His plans and timing are perfect, but we must be willing to wait.

Sarai told her husband, Abram, to sleep with her maidservant, Hagar. Now think about that for a moment. According to the modern world we live in, most of us would identify Sarai's command to her husband as if she had encouraged him to participate in an act of adultery. How could encouraging adultery be an appropriate solution to a problem? Obviously, it wasn't. However, we must remember that the customs during Sarai and Abram's time were viewed much differently than they are in our present-day era. A married woman who wasn't able to have children was often required to give one of her maidservants to her husband so a child could be conceived and an heir be born into their family. Nevertheless, even if that was the custom, we must remember that God knows our needs and He will provide for them as He sees fit. It's not our job to fit into society. It's God's job to place us wherever and however He sees fit. We must be willing to wait upon the Lord.

Sarai was desperate for results. She admitted taking the situation into her own hands when she stated, "Perhaps I can build a family through her" (Genesis 16:2b). Sarai was making reference to her maidservant, Hagar. Oh, that we would let God be the provider for our lives and not ourselves. This scenario reminds me of how distracted our minds can get when we let situations consume us. When we desperately desire personal outcomes and results, we quickly take control of situations that were never intended for us to be in control of in the first place. In our haste, we overlook possible consequences for our actions until it's too late and a price has to be paid for something we never even planned.

Abram agreed to Sarai's plan. He slept with Hagar and she conceived. Sarai became angry because her maidservant began to despise her once she became pregnant. As a result, Sarai chose to mistreat her maidservant and Hagar fled to the desert.

Do you see how nothing good has come out of this story since Sarai took the situation into her own hands? Sarai's job was to cry out to God and wait patiently upon Him for her next steps. It was not her job to control the situation. Sarai was responsible to simply walk through the situation while following God's lead. How often does that describe you and me?

There are countless times when we long for results more than we long for God and the outcomes are typically bleak. Controlling the outcomes of our personal desires usually turns into a disaster of one kind or another. When will we submit to the fact that God's ways are always better than ours? When will we learn to wait upon the Lord and trust that His timing is best? When will we accept the fact that, in many instances, "Rejection Equals Protection?" God sees and knows what lies before us. He knows our strengths and weaknesses and He desires to protect us. Rejection of a prayer request may be exactly what we need in order for God to protect our hearts and minds from unforeseeable outcomes that may bring us great disaster or discouragement.

As the story continues, we find that the Lord allowed Hagar to conceive a son through Abram and they named him Ishmael. Scripture tell us that Ishmael's hand would be against everyone, and everyone's hand would be against him. He would live in hostility toward all his brothers (Genesis 16:11-12).

If Sarai had known all this beforehand, I wonder just how desperate she would have been to have had a child. But the question isn't about Sarai. The question is about us. How many times have we found ourselves in a similar situation? How often do we long for results more than we long for God and take situations into our own hands? In many instances, we might agree that Sarai simply represents us.

PERCEPTION VS. PERSPECTIVE

We need to maintain a godly perspective and attitude while we wait, despite the constant wrestling we may encounter with our human thoughts and feelings.

From time to time in our home, my husband and I share this comment with each other, *"Perceptions aren't always realities."* While that can be true in many cases, we need to be more concerned about our *perspective* rather than our *perception*. Many times, our own personal perceptions are based upon our senses—the things we see, feel, touch, taste and hear. Typically, our personal perceptions are based upon three of those five senses ... what we see, hear and feel. However, those feelings aren't typically coming from our physical body. They come from our emotions. Everyone's emotions beat to a different drum so *BEWARE*! Due to that point alone, it's fair to say that in many instances, "Perceptions aren't always realities."

For example, just because I don't feel loved, doesn't mean that I'm not loved. Just because I don't feel blessed, doesn't mean that I'm not blessed. In order to have the right perception, we must have the right perspective. Those two ideas walk hand-in-hand with each other. The only right perspective for us to have comes from God Himself.

This is a critical point to consider as we relate it to the idea of waiting. The longer we wait for something, the more likely we are to get impatient and frustrated by a lack of results. The more impatient and frustrated we get over a lack of results, the more likely we are to begin to doubt. Doubting may result in us taking control of situations so we can get some favored results or outcomes that may not be possible if we continue to wait upon the Lord. We're so desperate for favored results that we start offering God our help and lose sight that our omnipotent God doesn't need our assistance, or interference, with His master plan and purpose for our lives.

We can't afford to let our emotions and feelings get in the way or they will distract us from maintaining a godly focus while we wait upon the Lord. The temptation to take control of a situation will become great and we'll find ourselves faced with a similar situation just like Sarai. She let her personal feelings and emotions carry her away to the point that she encouraged her husband to sleep with her maidservant. By taking the situation into her own hands, she had consequences to deal with and her own manipulation was her hardest "pregnancy-pill" to swallow. She struggled with anxiousness, which led to selfish motives. Our selfishness can lead to jealousy, anger, bitterness, resentment and even hatred. What ungodly characteristics!

We must be careful not to rush God's plans or promised blessings to us. There are reasons behind each of His ways. We must remember that

God is Sovereign. He can do whatever He pleases, whenever He pleases. Though we may never fully understand why God may choose to lead us down certain paths, we must trust that He knows what He's doing. After all, He is omniscient. He is our all-knowing God.

Sarai's number one problem was that she longed for a baby more than she longed for God. She clung to an earthly and temporal desire more than an eternal and spiritual one. In her moments of temptation, she longed to *have* a child rather than *be* a child of the one true God. That's a major problem, both for Sarai and for us. Isaiah 30:18b reminds us that, "Blessed are all who wait for Him!" We are first and foremost called to wait upon the Lord more than we wait upon anything, or anyone else in this world.

Be honest with yourself right now as you consider these next two questions. What are you truly longing for at this point in your life? Are you longing for the Lord, or are you longing for someone or something else? If it's anything other than the Lord, confess that to God. He already knows your heart. We can't run from God so why not be upfront and honest with Him? Doing so will actually allow you to be upfront and honest with yourself. In most cases, it's not God that we're running from. The reality is that we're trying to outrun ourselves, and we'll soon find that the run is futile. Don't be discouraged, be desperate. Become desperate for God. Long for Him as He longs for you. When God becomes the greatest desire of your heart, you will be willing to wait … regardless of the time … regardless of the cost.

Though the start of family life for Abram and Sarai wasn't ideal, we can learn an impactful lesson from this family's life as the years progressed. When Abram was 99 years old, God told him he would be the father of many nations. God also changed Abram's name to Abraham, and Sarai's name to Sarah. At that time, God promised Abraham that He would bless Sarah and give him a son through her. Abraham would name him Isaac.

What was so startling about the news was that this couple would bear their son when Abraham was 100 years old and Sarah was 90. That's

15 years after Sarai commanded Abram to sleep with Hagar. It's like they were merely kids back then! How incredible to know that Sarai's desperate desire to have a child was always in the will of God. A son had always been part of God's plan for her life. She simply needed to wait for it and long for God while she waited.

JESUS LONGED FOR GOD

The best example we have of a person who longed for God is Jesus Christ Himself. Jesus, God in flesh, came to this earth for 33 years with the intent to wait. He knew God's plans and purposes and He waited upon God's perfect timing to act on each one. He didn't wait wastefully, He waited purposefully. Jesus waited upon the Father by glorifying and honoring Him through His service. But what was Jesus really waiting for? Ultimately, He was waiting to die. What's even more incredible is that He was waiting to die *for us*. His death wasn't a benefit to Him. It was a benefit to us. Consider how painful His wait must have been as we reflect on His journey in His last days on earth.

Matthew 26 reveals the story of The Last Supper. At the table, among His disciples, the stage was set. Jesus shared the fact that Judas would be the one to betray Him into the hands of men. After they ate and drank together, they sang a hymn and went to the Mount of Olives where Jesus predicted Peter's denial. Then they went to a place called Gethsemane where Jesus agonized before he was betrayed by Judas. As He waited in the garden, He took a few men with Him and began to grieve. He admitted that His soul was overwhelmed with sorrow to the point of death.

Have you ever had to wait for something where you knew the outcome was going to be discouraging or disastrous? Maybe you became aware you were going to lose your job when economic times got tough. Maybe news reports predicted a natural disaster that resulted in a direct hit to your community and home where you lost everything. Maybe you had a loved one experience a terminal illness where you knew death awaited. The heartache, pain and sorrow in those types of situations can be overwhelming.

But what did Jesus do while He waited and grieved? Matthew 26:39 tells us that "he fell with his face to the ground and prayed." He chose to continue worshiping God by communing with Him. What did Jesus say amidst his sorrow? "My Father, if it is possible, may this cup be taken from me. Yet not as I will, but as you will."

As He prayed, He shared His heart with His Father. He expressed His deepest desire to not have to endure the cross. Not only did He plead this request once, He did it a second and a third time. That's what it means to petition to the Lord. We don't ask only once. We pour our hearts out to Him and ask again and again. But while we ask, we have a heart that's willing to receive any answer God brings. Though we pray, longing for the answer we desire, we have an even greater longing for God and we prepare ourselves for the answer He will reveal. Not our will, but His be done. That's what it means to have the right perspective.

What else is amazing about Jesus' life is what He longed for while He ministered during His time on earth. In Jesus' prayer found in John 17, it's evident that He longed for mankind to have eternal life. He prayed that man would know God, the only true God, and Jesus Christ, whom God had sent. He also longed that God would glorify Himself with the glory Jesus had with His Father before the world began.

Jesus waited selflessly. His heart's desire was that God would be glorified and man would be saved. He waited with passion and purpose. As He waited to die, He prayed that His death would be a benefit to others. Jesus knew all that was going to happen to Him. He wasn't looking forward to a gruesome death on the cross, yet He longed that the Scriptures would be fulfilled and that His Father would be glorified through Him. Jesus longed to make God known to the people of the world in order that the love of God would be in them, namely, Jesus. What a vision. What a focus. What a commitment. What a longing. What a wait.

Paul's Longing—To Know Christ

Another person who shared this longing was Paul. Paul considered everything to be a loss compared to the surpassing greatness of knowing Christ Jesus. The beginning of his bold statement from Philippians 3:10 makes his longing clear, "I want to know Christ." Does that represent the longing of our hearts? Do you and I long to glorify God by getting to know Jesus? Are we willing to persevere and press on for the prize that awaits us in heaven?

Philippians 3:20 clearly reminds believers that our citizenship is in heaven. You see, we are strangers and foreigners in this world. We don't fit in, nor are we supposed to fit in. But what should we do while we wait? How do we make the most of our earthly residence while we're here? We are to eagerly await a Savior from our heavenly home, the Lord Jesus Christ. We are to long for our heavenly prize.

When is the last time that you eagerly awaited to encounter Christ face-to-face? Sure, there are times when we get fed up with this world and we want out—now! However, are we eagerly awaiting to escape the difficulties of this world, or are we truly waiting to be united with Christ? That can be both a challenging and sobering thought. It's one that needs an honest evaluation.

Eagerly long for God. Be desperate for His return. Desire to share your testimony with the people God's placed in your life. Crave to grow in Him and be obedient to His call. Desire nothing more than Christ. Long for Him with eager anticipation as you wait. Long to be united with Christ.

DISCUSSION QUESTIONS:

1. Answer the first two questions on a scale of 1-10 (1=low, 10=high):

    a. How quick are you to rush, or interrupt, God's plans for your life when your wait time becomes long? _____

    b. How much would you say you trust God? _____

    c. Are your ratings for "a" and "b" similar or different? Explain.

    _____

    _____

    _____

    _____

2. Consider the phrase, *"Rejection Equals Protection."* Can you look back on your life and see times when God's answer to you may have been either "No" or "Wait" so that He could protect you? Share an example.

    _____

    _____

    _____

    _____

3. What is one thing that you're truly longing for at this point in your life?

    _____

    _____

    _____

    _____

a. Why do you believe your heart longs for that desire so greatly?

_____

_____

_____

_____

b. Do you believe that longing is from God or yourself? Why?

_____

_____

_____

_____

4. Have you ever longed for God in the same way that you've longed for personal desires in this world? Do you believe you need to grow in your longing for God more? Share your thoughts.

_____

_____

_____

_____

3

PRAY

THERE IS NO BETTER EXAMPLE for us to follow in terms of a prayer warrior than Jesus Christ Himself. Jesus' life revolved around being in constant communication with God.

We need to follow His example while we wait. Jesus waited 33 years on earth before being reunited with God the Father in heaven. How He longed to be with His Father. He was desperate for Him. Jesus was motivated by the fact that He would sit at the right hand of the Father again one day, but not until God's perfect plan on earth had been fulfilled.

So, what did Jesus do while He waited? He prayed. He made times to be quiet in lonely places just so He could converse with His Father. Often times we don't even know what to pray for, or what words to say when we pray. But Jesus was our example. He took every thought captive and made it obedient to God (2 Corinthians 10:5). Even when Jesus was in the wilderness being lured by Satan for 40 days and 40 nights, He spoke the written Word of God to ward off the devil's temptation.

What else did Jesus do while He waited to be reunited with God? He proclaimed the Good News of eternal life for those who would believe in Him alone for their salvation. He was an encouragement to others. He spoke the truth. He kept an eternal focus. He refrained from getting caught up with the things of this world. He served others in love. This type of a response is only possible when we keep in close fellowship and communion with God through prayer.

Jesus obviously knew His Father like no other. Jesus knew that prayer was an essential part of His relationship with God while living out His time here on earth. Prayer is what kept Jesus in direct fellowship and obedience with the Father.

Luke 5:16 says, "But Jesus often withdrew to lonely places and prayed." Notice that this verse doesn't say Jesus prayed because He was lonely. It was quite the contrary for Him. Crowds demanded His presence. People wanted to hear His words and be healed of their sicknesses. But Jesus knew He needed to set aside quiet times where He could simply commune with God alone. He treasured His relationship with His Father and was willing to put aside all other earthly responsibilities in order to maintain fellowship with the One He loved above all. Jesus knew He needed to prioritize the important aspects of eternal life over the urgent things in this physical life. Jesus' example of prayer demonstrated His longing for eternal values over earthly responsibilities.

Not only did Jesus withdraw to lonely places to pray, Luke 5:16 states that He did this *often*. Frequency, persistence and perseverance must be associated with an effective prayer life. We should never minimize our need to pray. We are challenged in 1 Thessalonians 5:17 to, "pray continually." Our prayers should be part of our everyday life and not only a desperate plea to God when disaster strikes. God has created us to fellowship with Him. Prayer is the key to making this happen. Waiting allows us a perfect opportunity to pray and draw closer to God while we wait for His direction in our lives.

THE PARABLE OF THE PERSISTENT WIDOW

We just referenced 1 Thessalonians 5:17, which reminded us to pray continually. To emphasize this idea, Jesus shared a parable with His disciples to show them that they should always pray and not give up. It's found in Luke 18:1-8.

In this story, there were two people. One was a judge who didn't fear God or care what people thought. The other was a widow. She lived in the same town and kept coming to the judge with a repetitive plea. Her plea was simply this, "Grant me justice against my adversary."

For some time, he refused her request. But as time went on, and the woman kept persistent with her plea to the judge, he eventually said to himself, "Even though I don't fear God or care about men, yet because this widow keeps bothering me, I will see that she gets justice, so that she won't eventually wear me out with her coming!" Isn't that interesting how her persistence got him to change his response to her? The judge wasn't only tired of the widow asking him the same request over and over again, he actually feared that she might exhaust him if he kept denying her the request.

Jesus reminded the disciples that God will bring justice for His chosen ones who cry out to Him day and night. He will not keep putting them off. If this judge, who didn't fear God or care about others, was willing to grant a request to a mere acquaintance, how much more is our loving Father willing to grant a request to His children?

Let me be honest. There are times when I've had good intentions of bringing my requests before the Lord, but I've gotten so caught up in life that I've unintentionally missed out on the actual step of praying. I've spent so much time *thinking* about my prayer that I've forgotten to actually pray. And thinking is altogether different from doing. Other times, I've taken my request to the Lord the very first time, but then that's been it. I don't go back repeatedly. I continue to think about my request in my head, or I talk about it with others, but I don't keep taking it to the Lord. I consider that a "one and done" mindset. Can you relate? If so, why do we do that? For me, I think it's the fact that I know God is omniscient. He knows all things. He knows what I'm thinking and He knows my needs. Because of that, I feel like I'm a broken record, a whiner and complainer, or a squeaky wheel if I keep going to Him with the same request over and over again. I don't want to be that kind of child before my King.

But I need to take on a different perspective. I need to remember that I am God's child. Children approach their parents for all kinds of things time and time again. They don't give up. They make their wants and desires known. They are persistent and they typically don't give up until they receive the answers they're hoping for. Though all of our desires won't be granted, there is certainly something to be said about the persistence of asking.

God wants us to come to Him in prayer with childlike faith as well. In a book called *A Praying Life*, by Paul Miller, the idea of praying like a child is addressed. We are reminded that little children never get frozen by their selfishness. They come just as they are, totally self-absorbed. They just say what's on their minds. They're real. They aren't artificial or hidden behind a mask. God understands that our lives are messy and He's open to receiving us that way. We can come to Him completely overwhelmed and with wandering minds. He welcomes that. God's not asking us to come before Him in perfection. He wants the real us to meet the real God.

God wants us to keep coming to Him, as He is the Source of all good things. He is meant to be our number one priority—always. Keep praying your heart to God, dear friends. Know that He hears, He sees and He understands. God is pleased when we commune with Him. Paul Miller shared that, "If we think we can do life on our own, we will not take prayer seriously. Our failure to pray will always feel like something else—a lack of discipline or too many obligations. But when something is important to us, we make room for it."

Prayer reminds us that we can't do life on our own. We need God's help and we must rely on His grace and mercy to get us through. Prayer keeps us completely dependent upon the Lord. There is no substitute for His presence. We pray to God because we trust Him and are confident in His love, protection and power. Those are reasons enough to keep praying, dear friends. Keep praying.

DAVID—"A MAN AFTER GOD'S OWN HEART"

As believers in Christ, prayer is vital to maintain a right relationship with God. It is our way of communicating with Him on a personal basis.

God desires for us to engage in a relationship with Him and He's given us the opportunity to exude our praise, thanksgiving, confession and requests to Him.

The more I learn about God's servant David, the more I understand why David was called, "a man after [God's] own heart" (Acts 13:22). Yes, David was a sinner just like you and me. Yes, David made terrible mistakes that some people in our world would consider unforgiveable. But one thing that separates David from so many other Christians is that his relationship with the Lord revolved around constant communication with each other.

This same relationship is available to each of us as followers of Christ, but most of us take it for granted. Only a small percentage of Christians truly appreciate the gift of communing with God enough to actually embrace this part of their spiritual relationship and grow close to God.

The book of Psalms illustrates numerous examples of how David communed and included God in his prayer life:

Praise:

- Psalm 27:1—"*The LORD is my light and my salvation—whom shall I fear? The LORD is the stronghold of my life—of whom shall I be afraid?*"

- Psalm 103:1-5—"*Praise the LORD, O my soul; all my inmost being, praise his holy name. Praise the LORD, O my soul, and forget not all his benefits—who forgives all your sins and heals all your diseases, who redeems your life from the pit and crowns you with love and compassion, who satisfies your desires with good things so that your youth is renewed like the eagle's.*"

Thanksgiving:

- Psalm 28:7—"The LORD is my strength and my shield; my heart trusts in him, and I am helped. My heart leaps for joy and I will give thanks to him in song."

- Psalm 107:1—"Give thanks to the LORD, for he is good; his love endures forever."

- Psalm 30:11-12—"You turned my wailing into dancing; you removed my sackcloth and clothed me with joy, that my heart may sing to you and not be silent. O LORD my God, I will give you thanks forever."

Confession:

- Psalm 25:7—"Remember not the sins of my youth and my rebellious ways; according to your love remember me, for you are good, O LORD."

- Psalm 25:11—"For the sake of your name, O LORD, forgive my iniquity, though it is great."

- Psalm 106:6—"We have sinned, even as our fathers did; we have done wrong and acted wickedly."

Request:

- Psalm 25:4-5—"Show me your ways, O LORD, teach me your paths; guide me in your truth and teach me, for you are God my Savior, and my hope is in you all day long."

- Psalm 31:2—"Turn your ear to me, come quickly to my rescue; be my rock of refuge, a strong fortress to save me."

- Psalm 106:4-5—"Remember me, O LORD, when you show favor to your people, come to my aid when you save them, that I may enjoy *the prosperity of your chosen ones, that I may share in the joy of your nation and join your inheritance in giving praise."*

David's life reflected a supernatural relationship with the Lord. He was willing to draw near to God through prayer. His prayers indicated the reverence, respect and trust he had for the Almighty God.

STEPHEN—PRAYED WHILE WAITING TO DIE

In Acts Chapter seven, we learn of Stephen (Acts 7:54-60). Stephen is described in the Bible as being a man full of faith and of the Holy Spirit. He was chosen as one of seven men to distribute food to the needy in the early church. Stephen was the first person to give up his life for the sake of the gospel. He was stoned to death for proclaiming Christ. Wow, consider that for a moment. Stephen was stoned to death. What a brutal way to die. Thankfully, that form of death isn't something most of us can even grasp. It overwhelms me to think of the painful and gruesome details associated with that type of death.

When I consider what Stephen must have endured, I can't help but wonder, "What were the last moments of his life like? How did he keep a godly focus? What did he do while he anticipated his death?" Acts 7:59 says, "While they were stoning him, Stephen prayed, 'Lord Jesus, receive my spirit.'" Isn't that incredible? As Stephen waited for his horrendous pain and torment to come to an end, he chose to pray. What a radical decision to make in desperate times. He prayed.

Would that decision be at the forefront of our minds if we were faced with a similar situation? How about right now as we are struggling through the difficulties of life? When we're at a dead end? When we're desperate for relief? When there seems to be no way out? Is prayer our first response? Do we choose to call out to the One who is able to receive our spirit?

Stephen did even more than just pray for the Lord to receive his spirit while he was waiting to die. During those final, excruciating moments of his life, he fell to his knees and cried out, "Lord, do not hold this sin against them" (Acts 7:60). Not only was Stephen willing to die for the sake of Christ, he was also willing to forgive his enemies while he was being killed. What a testimony of his love and faith in God.

It is truly a supernatural response to even consider prayer and forgiveness in our darkest moments. Yet it is a heart fully devoted to God that will actually carry out the act of praying and forgiving during desperate times. A response like Stephen's is only possible through the power of God, the work of the Holy Spirit, and our confidence in Jesus Christ, our Savior and Lord. Yes, we can choose to pray—even as we prepare to die.

Stephen's godly response was an exact imitation of Jesus' when He, too, was dying a slow, painful, gruesome death on the cross. When Jesus was crucified on the cross with two other criminals on either side of Him, He communed with His Father as well, saying, "Father, forgive them, for they do not know what they are doing" (Luke 23:34). Within only a few hours from that statement, Jesus called out with a loud voice saying, "Father, into your hands I commit my spirit. When He had said this, He breathed his last" (Luke 23:46).

Both Stephen and Jesus actively waited upon God during their final moments of earthly life until He determined the right time to receive their spirits. What will we do while we wait?

Discussion Questions:

1. Is prayer an active part of your spiritual life? YES NO (Circle one)

   a. If so, how would you describe your current prayer life? Do you truly pour your heart out to God or do you hold some things back? Explain.

   _____

   _____

   _____

   _____

   b. If not, what is holding you back? How would you be willing to start incorporating prayer into your life?

   _____

   _____

   _____

   _____

2. Are you more apt to pray when life is easy or when life is hard? Share your thoughts.

   _____

   _____

   _____

   _____

3. Consider a difficult circumstance you're currently facing:

    a. Have you taken it to the Lord in prayer?
        YES   NO   (Circle one)

    b. Are you praying for it repeatedly?
        YES   NO   (Circle one)

    c. What is God teaching you as you pray for it?

    _____

    _____

    _____

    _____

4. Why should prayer be important to you?

    _____

    _____

    _____

    _____

5. Have you ever seen prayer make a difference in your life? Explain.

    _____

    _____

    _____

    _____

4

INQUIRE OF GOD

IT'S A KNOWN FACT THAT asking questions is a great way of finding answers. However, asking questions typically requires a humble heart. When we ask a question, we're admitting that we don't know something. It means we need help. We need assistance. It means we're willing to rely on the knowledge of someone, or something, other than ourselves.

In today's society, asking questions is becoming a thing of the past. Why? Because we seem to have access to numerous, satisfying answers right at our fingertips. Instead of asking for directions, we can plug a street address into our GPS and have an electronic voice lead us to our destination. Instead of asking someone for a recipe, we can go to the Internet and plug in the name of a favorite dish or dessert. With the touch of a button, the computer can conveniently generate a 4"x 6" recipe card where all of the necessary ingredients and directions magically appear. Instead of going to a doctor and asking them to identify an ailment we've been suffering from for any length of time, many of us are quick to type in our symptoms online and allow a website to generate a suggested diagnosis. If we aren't content with the results, we have the liberty of going to other websites until we get the responses that pacify our minds.

Though most answers for us are just a quick click away, ponder this thought with me for a moment. When we have questions, do we crave the *right* answers, or do we crave *immediate* and *satisfying* answers? There's a big difference between the two and we must be careful as to which option we choose.

You see, we live in a "have it your way" and "have it now" society. Fast food drive-thrus, pay-at-the-pump gas stations and self-checkout grocery stores remind us that we're people who are constantly in a hurry. We can't afford to waste time waiting around. We crave speed and convenience. We're becoming desensitized to the idea of having to wait for almost anything. We no longer want to wait because we don't have to wait. While there are great things regarding our ability to get answers in a flash, is that doing us more harm than good? We're so quick and desperate to find answers that we hardly allow enough time to settle in before determining if what we really *wanted* in that moment was indeed what we truly *needed* overall. Are we letting the urgent things of life rule over the important things of life?

One of the greatest things about waiting is that it gives us time to determine how much we really want something. Immediacy doesn't teach us how to long for things. If God answered all of our questions as fast as the Internet did, we'd never need to long for Him and His best for us. Waiting teaches us how to have a humble heart. But what does a humble heart look like? In order to answer that question, let's first consider the word humility.

Some people understand the word humility to mean that we should think lowly of ourselves. However, that's not the correct interpretation. We don't need to think less of ourselves. We need to think of ourselves less. We need to think more of others. Humility is unselfish. Humility puts the needs of others before our own. When we have a humble heart we lack a natural, sinful quality—pride. When we lack pride, we supernaturally gain a spirit of submission.

Humility is necessary in order for us to have the attitude of a servant. A servant's attitude reflects the heart of Christ. As the Scriptures state in Philippians 2:3-4, "Do nothing out of selfish ambition or vain conceit, but in humility consider others better than yourselves. Each of you should look not only to your own interests, but also to the interests of others."

MARY AND JONAH IDENTIFIED WITH GOD

One of the verses I treasure most in Scripture reflects the words of Mary, the mother of Jesus. After the angel Gabriel shared with her that she had found favor with God, he went on to explain how she would bear the Son of the Most High God as a virgin. Mary's humble response is reflected in Luke 1:38 when she graciously replied, "I am the Lord's servant. May it be to me as you have said."

Mary's response demonstrated humility for two reasons. I will touch on the first reason now and reflect on the second reason later in the book when we discuss the idea of trusting God.

The initial words of Luke 1:38 boldly declare who Mary claimed to be. Mary identified herself as being the Lord's servant. A servant is known as a person being in a position of submission to another who is in authority over them. A servant has a master. It is the Person who Mary acknowledged in the first few words of her response that is far more profound than what she defined of her own position. You see, she called herself a servant. But she wasn't just anyone's servant. She was the Lord's servant. Submitting to God as her ultimate authority, Mary was most willing to abide by the words spoken to her from the angel of the Lord.

What a remarkable response after being told such mind-boggling news. Her heart was prepared to hear from God. Mary wasn't being asked if she wanted to become the mother of Jesus, she had simply been given a special assignment from God Himself. She wasn't asked to take time to wait, pray and think things over until she was ready to give a sound decision of her own. She was expected to reply with confirmation regarding what the angel told her. That is exactly what she did by having a heart that anticipated a godly response to her Master's call.

It is our human nature to want to stand alone and receive glory for whatever we can. It is more difficult to identify ourselves with another person we respect and then share in only half of the glory that may come our way. It is completely unnatural to identify ourselves with another person we respect and give them *all* the praise and glory for something that comes our way. But when we align ourselves with God, we are living a supernatural life. There is no longer anything natural about it. God deserves any and all praise for the good that results from having our lives aligned with Christ. Identifying ourselves with Him is necessary in order for us to give Him extravagant praise.

Though we are to be humble in spirit, we are also told to boast in the Lord. While that may seem like an oxymoron, to be humble and yet boast, it is exactly what God calls us to do. First Corinthians 1:30-31 says, "It is because of him that you are in Christ Jesus, who has become for us wisdom from God—that is, our righteousness, holiness and redemption. Therefore, as it is written: 'Let him who boasts, boast in the Lord.'" Aren't those profound words? It is because of God that we are able to be in a relationship with Christ. It is Christ who is our wisdom from God. He is our righteousness, holiness and redemption. We are nothing of ourselves, but having aligned ourselves with God, we get to experience it all. Praise the Lord!

Jonah is another person of the Bible who verbally identified himself with God. However, the difference between Mary and Jonah comes when we see *at what point* they identified themselves with the Living God.

Remember, while Mary submitted to God's calling for her life, Jonah ran. He ran after hearing God's command for him to go to Nineveh. He boarded a ship headed to Tarshish and a violent storm arose. The sailors cast lots to determine who was responsible for the catastrophe they were experiencing. When the lot fell on Jonah, they asked him, "Tell us, who is responsible for making all this trouble for us? What do you do? Where do you come from? What is your country? From what people are you?" (Jonah 1:8). Though the sailor's questions were many, the words to Jonah's answer were few. He simply said, "I am a Hebrew and I worship the Lord, the God of heaven, who made the sea and the land" (vs 9). This response terrified them.

Let's look at our own lives for a moment. How quick are we to verbally align ourselves with the Lord when we are among other people? Are we willing to identify ourselves with the Lord no matter who is around us, or are we selective as to whom we share that key information with so we don't suffer any consequences? If someone asked, "Who are you?" would our immediate response be, "We are Christians and we worship the Lord?"

If we have accepted Jesus Christ as our personal Lord and Savior by receiving the free gift of salvation by the grace of God through the shed blood of Jesus Christ on the cross of Calvary, then we have entered into a blood relationship with Him. We are part of His family. There is nothing anyone or anything can do to separate us from the love of Christ. If we have entered into a relationship with Him, we now have a new identity. We are no longer of ourselves. We are of God. If we are of God then we should have a desire to proclaim the new identity we have in Christ.

We have been bought with a price ... the ultimate price. We are new creations. We have the fullness of God in us. We are identified by Christ alone. We must be humble as we willingly submit and align ourselves with the risen Lord. There is no greater privilege in life than to be identified with Christ. This is God's free gift to us and we are to boast in Him. I am His and He is mine. Hallelujah! Praise the Lord!

DAVID COMMUNED WITH GOD

David is referenced in Scripture as being, "a man after [God's] own heart" (Acts 13:22). What an amazing description for God to give another human being. David was a sinner like all of us, yet he walked with God and found favor in the Lord's sight.

A key component to any growing relationship is communication. Relationships require the contribution of two or more people in order to function properly. David understood the importance of this in regards to his relationship with the Lord. David practiced being in constant communication with God. David knew that in order to receive direction from God, he needed to be diligent in the area of inquiring of God. In first and second Samuel, we find multiple conversations David had as he waited upon the Lord before taking his next step of faith:

- "When David was told, 'Look, the Philistines are fighting against Keilah and are looting the threshing floors,' *he inquired of the LORD*, saying, 'Shall I go and attack these Philistines?' The LORD answered him, 'Go, attack the Philistines and save Keilah'" (1 Samuel 23:1-2).

- "Once again *David inquired of the LORD*, and the LORD answered him, 'Go down to Keilah, for I am going to give the Philistines into your hand'" (1 Samuel 23:4).

- "...and *David inquired of the LORD*, 'Shall I pursue this raiding party? Will I overtake them?' 'Pursue them,' he answered. 'You will certainly overtake them and succeed in the rescue'" (1 Samuel 30:8).

- "In the course of time, *David inquired of the LORD*. 'Shall I go up to one of the towns of Judah?' he asked. The LORD said, 'Go up.' David asked, 'Where shall I go?' 'To Hebron,' the LORD answered'" (2 Samuel 2:1).

- "So *David inquired of the LORD*, 'Shall I go and attack the Philistines? Will you hand them over to me?' The LORD answered him, 'Go, for I will surely hand the Philistines over to you'" (2 Samuel 5:19).

- "Once more the Philistines came up and spread out in the Valley of Rephaim; so *David inquired of the LORD*, and he answered, 'Do not go straight up, but circle around behind them and attack them in front of the balsam trees. As soon as you hear the sound of marching in the tops of the balsam trees, move quickly, because that will mean the LORD has gone out in front of you to strike the Philistine army'" (2 Samuel 5:22-24).

David wasn't merely *walking* with God. He understood the importance of *talking* with God as well. When we talk with someone, it's a two-way street. Conversations require a minimum of two people. We aren't expected to do all the talking ourselves. We talk as well as listen to what the other person has to say. This should hold true in our relationship with God as well. Like David, we are expected to bring our praises, thanksgiving, confession, petitions and requests before the Lord. However, we must also take time to listen to His responses to us. Those responses may be immediate, or they may take varying lengths of time before we hear from the Lord.

We can learn another important lesson from David found in 1 Samuel 22:3. While David escaped to a cave in order to spare his life from the angry and bitter King Saul, David's family came to be with him. They moved on to Moab and David asked the king, "Would you let my father and mother come and stay with you until I learn what God will do for me?"

The second half of that verse is key for us to learn from when it says, "…until I [David] learn what God will do for me." What an amazing phrase! David was willing to take whatever time was needed to wait and learn how his next steps were being directed by the Lord. Wow! What a godly example we have through the life of David. God will work out the details if we are simply willing to wait for His plans to be revealed to us. The question becomes, "Are we willing to wait as long as it takes until we receive direction from the Lord?" Be careful, dear friends, not to rush your wait.

SAUL'S REBELLION AGAINST GOD

Now let's take a moment to look at the life of Saul. If the question was asked as to why Saul died, many would respond by saying that Saul took his own life after being pursued and wounded by the Philistines. He fell on his own sword to prevent himself from being abused by his attackers (1 Chronicles 10:1-5). Fear and insecurity certainly played a key role as to why Saul was encouraged to take his own life. However, the sole reason Saul died is found in 1 Chronicles 10:13-14. It says, "Saul died because he was unfaithful to the LORD; he did not keep the word of the LORD and even consulted a medium for guidance, and did not inquire of the

LORD. So, the LORD put him to death and turned the kingdom over to David son of Jesse."

Even though it was Saul himself who took his own sword to fall upon and die, it was the Lord who put Saul to death. It was not his attackers ... it was not Saul ... it was the Lord God Almighty.

I'm not sure about you, but I was astonished after reading 1 Chronicles 10:13-14, specifically because there were three defined points listed within those two verses that indicated the disobedient heart of Saul:

- He was unfaithful to the Lord

- He consulted a medium for guidance (i.e. a witch)

- He did not inquire of the Lord

Those were serious acts of rebellion, dear friends. While we may shake our heads and cast judgment on Saul for making such poor choices against the Lord's will, we need to ask ourselves if these same issues reflect our own hearts at times. Let's be honest with ourselves, and with the Lord, as we pick these issues apart and apply them to our own lives.

First, are we being faithful to the Lord while we wait upon Him? God's Word tells us to obey His commands. His Word tells us to hide God's Word in our hearts. His Word tells us to take every thought captive and make it obedient to Christ. His Word tells us to love one another. His Word tells us to be still and know that He is God. These commandments apply whether we are in a joyous or frustrating period of waiting. God expects our hearts to reflect faithfulness upon Him while we wait, despite the pleasant or difficult waiting patterns we experience.

Second, we see that Saul consulted a medium for guidance rather than inquire of the Lord. Now, while many would say that they would never consult a witch in their decision-making process, how many of us might seek consultation by means of another person or thing other than the Lord Himself? For example, how many of us have run to seek guidance or opinions from friends, family members or counselors before consulting God first? How many seek out a best-selling book, magazine article, recent survey or poll? How many look to horoscopes? How many of us watch the examples of what other people are doing around us and simply decide to follow in their footsteps because it looks like things have worked out for them?

If we are not consulting God for His wisdom, guidance and direction while we wait, then we are struggling with the same issue as Saul. God commands this of us, "But seek first his kingdom and his righteousness, and all these things will be given to you as well" (Matthew 6:33). God doesn't just want us to seek Him at some point while we are in a waiting pattern. He wants us to seek Him *first*. Many times, we pat ourselves on the back simply because we sought after God at some point during our waiting journey. But God is clear that He wants us to seek Him first ... not second ... not third ... not at some point ... but first!

This idea ties in with the very first commandment God clearly lays out for us in Exodus 20:3, "You shall have no other gods before me." Nothing is to come before God in our lives. He expects us to make Him our number one priority and He expects us to keep Him in that number one spot without exception. He is our ultimate authority and resource. He is to be our first "go-to" for all things. Running to anyone or anything before running to God is blatant disobedience.

However, allow me to share some encouraging news with you. We serve a God full of grace and mercy. Synonyms for the word *full* include: complete, bursting and chock-full. This means that His grace and mercy never runs out. God is always functioning at 100 percent. He can't ever be less than full.

Because God desires to be in a relationship with us, He has given us the opportunity to experience the fullness of God in our lives through the shed blood of Jesus Christ and the power of the Holy Spirit. He desires to pour out His grace and mercy on each one of His children. If we are willing to let God examine our lives and show us areas where we're struggling to put Him first, God grants us permission to confess that to Him so we can receive the fullness of His forgiveness for our sin.

God's forgiveness results in cleansing us from all unrighteousness (1 John 1:9). However, He doesn't only forgive us. In return, God gives us a purified heart so we can, once again, prioritize Him in our lives. We are not hopeless, dear friends. We have hope and victory residing in us. His name is Jesus. He is the Almighty God. Determine in your heart to put Him first in your life and let Him reign.

DISCUSSION QUESTIONS:

1. Philippians 2:3-4 says, *"Do nothing out of selfish ambition or vain conceit, but in humility consider others better than yourselves. Each of you should look not only to your own interests, but also to the interests of others."*

   a. How are you doing in the area of considering others better than yourself? Is it easy for you to look to the interests of others? Why or why not?

   _____

   _____

   _____

   _____

   b. Where do you see areas of opportunity in order for you to live these verses out to an even greater extent than you are living them out right now? Explain.

   _____

   _____

   _____

   _____

2. When God provides a command or direction on your life, are you more apt to respond like Mary or Jonah? Is it your tendency to submit to God (like Mary), or run from Him (like Jonah)? Why?

   _____

   _____

   _____

   _____

3. When you are around other people, are you quick to identify yourself with the Lord in your conversation with them, or are you hesitant to do so? Explain.

_____

_____

_____

_____

4. According to 1 Samuel 22:3, David was willing to wait until he, "*learned what God would do for [him].*"

    a. Does that response reflect how you wait upon the Lord? Share your thoughts.

_____

_____

_____

_____

    b. Are you quick to consult other people or things before inquiring of the Lord? If so, what are they and why do you gravitate to them?

_____

_____

_____

_____

5. Do you struggle to prioritize God first in your life? If so, what is your number one priority right now, and how would you be willing to make adjustments so God becomes your first priority?

_____

_____

_____

_____

5

ACCEPT THE WAIT

IN JOHN 18, WHEN JESUS had been betrayed by Judas, and the soldiers came to arrest Him, Simon Peter drew his sword and cut off the right ear of Malchus, the high priest's servant. Jesus commanded Peter, "Put your sword away! Shall not I drink the cup the Father has given me?" (John 18:11)

I find the words of that last sentence to be profound. "Shall not I drink the cup the Father has given me?" If we look back at verse 4 of John 18, we see that Jesus knew all that was going to happen to Him. He knew He was going to be betrayed by Judas. He knew the gruesome crucifixion that awaited Him. He knew that this experience would glorify the Father. But it wasn't the fact that Jesus *knew* what would happen to Him that was so extraordinary. It was the fact that He *accepted* God's plan for His life to the point that He was willing to endure it. God's plan for His Son would be difficult. It would be gruesome and painful. It would bring about physical death for Jesus. Yet He knew it was necessary. Jesus' physical death would open the door to the gift of spiritual life for the rest of the world. Jesus selflessly accepted God's perfect plan for His life, despite the pain and hardship that awaited.

Now let's make one point very clear here. Just because we accept something, doesn't mean we have to like it. Scripture never alludes to the fact that Jesus was happy and excited to bear the cross for the sin of the world. Not at all. As a matter of fact, we read in Luke 22:44 that, "Being in anguish, he [Jesus] prayed more earnestly, and his sweat was like drops of blood falling to the ground." So how would we describe the state Jesus was in at that point? Let's be honest. A person who is happy or excited doesn't typically sweat drops of blood. Jesus was in anguish over the weight of sin that lay before Him on the cross. He didn't want to endure the cross, but He knew He had to do it. That was part of God's perfect plan for His life. That's how God would demonstrate His love to us. While we were sinners, Christ chose to die for us. Jesus glorified God by obeying His Father to the point of death ... death on a cross. Jesus came to earth and accomplished God's purpose for His life. That purpose was to glorify God the Father by bringing the gift of salvation to the world. And that's exactly what Jesus did. He accepted the will of His Father.

God gave His Son, Jesus, a *cup* to drink. That cup was a specific assignment for Jesus to fulfill. His assignment was to live a perfect life and die a gruesome death so that all might be saved. While Jesus waited for the day of His betrayal by Judas, which would then lead to His arrest and crucifixion, He accepted what each day brought Him until the Scriptures would be fulfilled. He determined to glorify God no matter how painful or long the wait became. He knew God had a perfect plan for His life and He knew God had an appointed time for every assignment He gave to Jesus.

This concept is no different for us as children of God. The Lord has a specific plan and purpose for our lives, just as He did for Jesus. Our specific assignments may look different than the ones that Jesus carried out, but the idea behind them is all the same. We are to glorify God by living in obedience to His unique calling on our lives. We don't have to like it, we simply need to live it. And we can only live it out if we accept His perfect plan for us individually ... including the difficult, and sometimes painful, times of waiting.

It's likely that many of us have, or will, become impatient while we wait simply because we want an answer—and we want it now! We don't like the time factor involved in waiting. However, if we're not willing to put the appropriate wait time in, in order to receive an answer, we will likely miss the answer altogether.

Let me share a personal example to emphasize this point. I recently purchased a Bible study that I was excited to teach for the upcoming summer. When I submitted my order, I received a notice that the Bible study kit I ordered was on backorder. I felt my blood pressure rise a bit as I had ordered this study on the very first day it had been released. "How can it already be on backorder?" Well, no matter how many times I asked myself that same question, the result was the same. I would have to wait for it if I eventually wanted to receive it.

In my excitement and impatience, I decided to check my order status the next day. (I must have thought my order might have miraculously shipped overnight!) As I looked at my order status online, I saw an area on the company's website that allowed me the option to be involved in an online chat with one of their customer service representatives to help answer any of my questions. Since I was eager to find out how long my order would take before it shipped, I began typing to an online agent right away.

As my fingers rapidly typed out the letters that formulated the words to my question, I submitted my text into "outer space" and anxiously awaited a response from the other end. Unfortunately for me, there was always a delay of several minutes from the time the agent received my question until I received their response. As we carried on our conversation, I realized how unfair it was that I was promptly responding to their questions to me, yet they seemed to be taking their own sweet time replying to mine. The funniest part of it all was when I realized that I was the one who seemed to be demonstrating the better customer service between the two of us, and that wasn't even my job. My quick response times made me feel like I was doing the other person's job when I was simply the customer eager for answers.

As some of the wait times grew longer and longer, I knew that I was at the mercy of the customer service agent, Donnie, to answer my questions.

No matter how long it took him to respond, I had to wait and simply anticipate that a reply would indeed come from him—eventually.

Now, I am a doer by nature, and it drives me crazy to sit around and wait for things when I know I could be productive doing something else. So, after the first couple of typing interactions I had with Donnie, I realized that I could get a little something done around the house while I waited for his response. Since I had a baby shower gift to wrap, I decided to go downstairs to find a gift bag and tissue paper so I could neatly wrap my present while I was on hold waiting for a response from my agent. But an interesting thing happened as I took on this additional responsibility while I waited.

After sending my most recent reply off to Donnie, I quickly ran downstairs to get my gift supplies. When I came up just a few short moments later and looked to see what my agent wrote, there was a note on my computer that said, "Due to a delayed response time by you, your chat time with your agent has ended." I was frustrated. "What?!?! Are you kidding me?!?!" I walked away for two whole minutes, and I'm the one who got cut off from the agent. How come I had to wait for nearly five minutes for him to reply to my emails, yet I was expected to respond to his emails in a matter of seconds? How is that fair?!?!"

However, the more I thought about that experience, the more I kept reflecting on my relationship with God. I come to Him with my prayers and petitions and I need to be willing to give God as much or little time as He desires to answer my pleas. However, He expects me to be attentive to Him. If I really want an answer bad enough, I'll wait as long as it takes to receive His response and I will not lose focus, or patience, in the process because He is the giver of all good things, even if the package of the good thing doesn't look so pretty to me.

Though we typically hope for an immediate answer from God, only He knows the perfect timing for the response He will give us. Knowing that His response will be perfect, we need to be patient, yet ready to receive His reply. God's timing is never early and will never be late. There is a time for everything that's necessary for us in God's eyes. Be willing to wait for His answer patiently. At the same time, be just as willing to respond to His answer quickly.

As God promises in Jeremiah 33:3, "Call to me and I will answer you and tell you great and unsearchable things that you do not know." God will answer His children and His answer will include great and hidden things. Do you believe that? The things God will reveal to us will be new because He says in this verse that they are things that we have not known. Does that excite you enough to call out to Him? We need to wait for His response. If we don't, we'll be the ones who miss out. The great and mighty things God has in store for us are always worth the wait.

The Testing of Job

Job is a man in the Bible who is known as being blameless and upright. He feared God and shunned evil. What an incredible description for a human being living in a fallen world. However, just because Job was known as being blameless and upright doesn't mean that he didn't sin. Scripture is clear to point out that, "All have sinned and fall short of the glory of God" (Romans 3:23). "There is none righteous, no not one" (Romans 3:10). However, despite the fact that Job was born into sin like the rest of us, he was a man who feared God and shunned evil.

As we learn about Job's life from the beginning of his story, we learn that he was married and had seven sons and three daughters. He was a man blessed with great wealth. He owned seven thousand sheep, three thousand camels, five hundred yoke of oxen and five hundred donkeys. He also had a large number of servants. He was the greatest man among all the people of the East (Job 1:1-4).

One day, Satan and the angels presented themselves before God. When the Lord asked where they had come from, Satan said they had been roaming through the earth and going back and forth in it. God then asked them, "Have you considered my servant Job? There is no one on earth like him; he is blameless and upright, a man who fears God and shuns evil" (Job 1:8).

I find it so interesting that Satan and his angels had not even asked God if they could put Job to the test. It was God Himself who suggested it. Does that seem right? Job was a man of integrity. As far as we know, he hadn't done anything wrong to deserve punishment. It was like God had chosen to punish him for no reason. Is that fair? But this is where we struggle. We see situations from our perspective rather than God's and we determine what's right or wrong based on having the wrong viewpoint.

Job was a man who feared God. We must remember that God loves those who fear Him so we know that He loved Job. God wasn't punishing him. He was testing him. There's a big difference between the two. God tests those He loves. From our perspective, that can seem a bit confusing. Why wouldn't God just keep showering blessings on those who live godly lives?

Discipline is far different than punishment. It is associated with testing. We must be careful to keep the right definition in mind as we consider its meaning. The purpose of discipline is to teach, train, guide and instruct. God's intent for disciplining His children is to grow and mature us, not intimidate or shun. The latter refers to the idea of punishment. Discipline should draw us closer to God, not farther from Him.

God's Word provides us with several verses to encourage us on how we should view discipline in order to not lose heart. Take time to meditate on each one.

Hebrews 12:6

*"... the Lord disciplines those he loves, and he
punishes everyone he accepts as a son."*

Hebrews 12:7

*"Endure hardship as discipline; God is treating you as
sons. For what son is not disciplined by his father?"*

Proverbs 3:11-13

*"My son, do not despise the Lord's discipline and do not
resent his rebuke, because the Lord disciplines those he loves,
as a father the son he delights in. Blessed is the man who
finds wisdom, the man who gains understanding, ..."*

Looking back at the story of Job, let's identify the multiple ways in which God allowed him to be tested by Satan and the angels. To most of us, we would consider Job's tests to be abrupt and overwhelming. The tests would've seemed virtually impossible for any of us to pass. Here's what happened.

In a single day, Job lost much of what was near and dear to him. The Sabeans attacked and carried off his oxen and donkeys. In the same day, fire burned up his sheep and servants. Then the Chaldeans formed three raiding parties and swept the area carrying off Job's camels while putting his servants to the sword. Shortly after, Job learned that a mighty wind from the desert struck the four corners of the house where his sons and daughters were feasting. The house collapsed on them and they all died.

What overwhelming circumstances. The difficulty kept coming, one after another. There wasn't even time for him to grasp the first devastation before the next one occurred. How did Job respond to such difficulty? How did his anger not burn against the Lord? How did He stay hopeful when he must have felt so hopeless?

His response was truly amazing. Scripture tells us that Job fell to the ground in worship. Despite all the hardship and devastation he'd been through, Job chose to worship God. Wow! What a testimony of trusting the Lord and accepting whatever God brought his way in order for the Lord to glorify Himself through Job. What a godly perspective this man had. We have so much to learn from his response. We must take our eyes off our circumstances and place them back on God. That's the only way to endure such pain.

Job knew that God was the One who had blessed him with his family, wealth and possessions. It was nothing Job had done of himself. He acknowledged that he came into this world with nothing. He understood that he would leave this world with nothing as well. He shared a perfect acceptance of this concept when he stated, "The LORD gave and the LORD has taken away; may the name of the LORD be praised" (Job 1:21b). That, my friends, is how we endure the difficulties of life. We remember that the Lord is sovereign. The Lord does as He pleases and we must accept whatever He gives or takes away. Having this perspective allowed Job to honor God and maintain his integrity. Job did not sin through his hardships by charging God with wrongdoing. Oh, that we would learn to respect and revere God in the same way. We certainly can, but the question is, "Will we?"

As if the hardships of that first day weren't enough, God allowed Satan and the angels to test him again, knowing that Job would maintain his integrity. God would let the evil ones strike his flesh and bones, but they were not permitted to take his life. So, they afflicted Job with painful sores from the soles of his feet to the top of his head. Keep in mind the descriptive words used here. These weren't just sores. They were described as painful sores all over his body.

I'm not sure about you, but when I get any type of severe bodily pain, it can wear me down in a hurry. I can be quick to grumble, complain and become short-tempered if I'm not careful. I can't even imagine what it would be like to be in physical pain from head to toe. We're told that Job took a piece of broken pottery and scraped himself with it as he sat among the ashes. Picture that. He quietly tended to his needs while sitting through the pain. It doesn't say he grumbled. It doesn't say he complained. It doesn't say he blamed God. It says he sat and scraped. We aren't made aware that he ever made a sound.

Not only did Job have to deal with his own thoughts and emotions as he struggled through the pain, he also had to endure a selfish, angry wife who spoke foolishness in his time of need. She questioned him by saying, "Are you still holding on to your integrity? Curse God and die!"

How's that for comfort and support when you need it most? The person who should have been spurring him on in his darkest moments was the one trying to get him to take his eyes off of the Lord. How discouraging.

When faced with his wife's challenging words, Job replied, "Shall we accept good from God, and not trouble?" What a response. His words were so profound. Job knew that he needed to accept both good and troubling situations from the Lord. Neither one should alter his focus or reverence for God.

How about you and me? Are we willing to accept troubling things from God just as easily as we accept good things from God? Does our perception of God change when we're walking in the ways of the Lord and He suddenly allows human disaster to strike ... possibly one after another? Do we want to curse God and die when we're faced with the impossible, or do we accept that He is growing and maturing us into the likeness of His image?

We're reminded in Hebrews 12:11 that, "No discipline seems pleasant at the time, but painful. Later on, however, it produces a harvest of righteousness and peace for those who have been trained by it."

Job's responses reflect a man who kept his eyes fixed on God rather than the things of this world. Job lost practically everything in a matter of two separate days, yet nothing made him lose his focus on his Sovereign Lord. That's why God gave him the tests. It wasn't because He wanted Job to suffer. It was because He desired to make Job savor God even more than before.

Maybe you're going through a period of waiting or hardship right now that seems to have no end in sight. Maybe you're at the brink of giving up. Maybe you feel like you've lost all hope. Hang on, dear friends. You may feel helpless, but you can remain hopeful. Remember that the Lord gives and takes away. May you choose to continue praising the Lord despite which path He brings your way. In your difficulty, choose not to sin. Choose to accept the wait. Accept the hardship as a way of God growing you to become more like Him. There is beauty in the wait, but you must be willing to wait for it.

DISCUSSION QUESTIONS:

1. Jeremiah 33:3 says, *"Call to me and I will answer you and tell you great and unsearchable things you do not know."*

   a. How often do you call out to God? Do you call out to Him even when you think you know the answers to things, or only when you're discouraged or are desperate for answers? Why?

   _____

   _____

   _____

   _____

   b. Do you believe that when you call out to God, He will answer you? Why or why not?

   _____

   _____

   _____

   _____

   c. As Jeremiah 33:3 states, do you believe God's answer to you will include great and hidden things? Does that excite you or intimidate you? Explain.

   _____

   _____

   _____

   _____

2. Job was a man who loved the Lord, yet God allowed much affliction, destruction and devastation to strike him. What are your thoughts on that? How does that make you view God?

   _____

   _____

   _____

   _____

3. How do you respond when you've been walking with the Lord and hardships come your way? Do you grumble and complain, lash out in anger against God, or do you accept the test? Explain.

_____

_____

_____

_____

4. How can you grow in the area of accepting long periods of waiting, or other hardships, that God allows you to undergo? What practical things can you do to keep your mind focused on God rather than on your hardships?

_____

_____

_____

_____

5. Hebrews 12:11 says, "_No discipline seems pleasant at the time, but painful. Later on, however, it produces a harvest of righteousness and peace for those who have been trained by it._" Are you willing to be trained by the Lord regardless of the discipline He brings into your life? Share your thoughts.

_____

_____

_____

_____

6

TRUST GOD

LET'S GO BACK AND LOOK at the second half of 1 Samuel 22:3 that we referenced in Chapter 4. It says, "...until I [David] learn what God will do for me." The last two words of that verse are significant. They may seem small and insignificant, but they are impactful. These two tiny words are the last two words stated by David when he said, *"for me."* David knew there was nothing he could do to please God based on his own wisdom, strength and power. Therefore, he relied fully upon God for the Lord's ultimate leading in his life. That meant that David would not take his next step until he learned what it was that God wanted him to do.

This is exactly the type of relationship we are to have with God. Just like David, we are expected to wait until we learn what God will do for us in different situations. Does this currently describe you and me? Do we wait patiently after inquiring of the Lord, knowing that He hears, He sees and He answers? Or do we rush into decisions before consulting God and hearing His response? He is able, dear friends. He is faithful and He will carry out *His* will for our lives. We simply need to trust in the truth of what we already know about God while we wait to find out His next step for our lives. Use your wait time to learn what God will do for you and be ready because He *will* do it. However, the timing of *when* He will do it and the exact way of *how* He will do it, must be left up to God.

SHADRACH, MESHACH AND ABEDNEGO

A great biblical example of some men who trusted in God is found in Daniel 3. It's the story of Shadrach, Meshach and Abednego. These three Jewish men had been put in charge over the affairs of the province of Babylon during the reign of King Nebuchadnezzar.

During this time, the king made an image of gold that was ninety feet high and nine feet wide. Nebuchadnezzar proclaimed that all people and nations were to fall down and worship the image of gold that had been set up whenever they heard the sound of the horn, flute, zither, lyre, harp, pipes and all kinds of music. The people were threatened. Anyone who chose not to fall down and worship the image would immediately be thrown into a blazing furnace, where death awaited.

Let's pause for a moment to consider a thought. I find it interesting that there is only one letter that separates the object King Nebuchadnezzar made all of the people worship compared to the object that Shadrach, Meshach and Abednego worshiped. It's the letter "L." While the king was determined to have his people worship an impressively large hunk of *gold*, the three men were determined in their hearts to worship their invisible, yet all-powerful, *God*. Isn't it amazing how one letter in our English language can change an entire word to take on a radically different meaning, which can change the entire focus of a situation?!

Now back to the story ...

When it was brought to King Nebuchadnezzar's attention that the three men would not pay attention to his command of serving his gods and worshiping the image of gold, the king became furious with rage. The king summoned the men and gave them a second chance to worship the gold image. At the same time, he was sure to restate the consequence that lie before the men if they chose to worship the Lord alone, reminding them that they would immediately be thrown into a blazing furnace. But Shadrach, Meshach and Abednego refused to submit.

King Nebuchadnezzar mocked the men by saying, "Then what god will be able to rescue you from my hand?" Do you see the control that the king thought he had over the men by ending his sentence with "my hand?" At this point, the king had no idea of the powerful right hand of God that supersedes the strength of any human hand. But proud King Nebuchadnezzar was soon to find out.

Shadrach, Meshach and Abednego bravely replied to the king, "O Nebuchadnezzar, we do not need to defend ourselves before you in this matter. If we are thrown into the blazing furnace, the God we serve is able to save us from it, and he will rescue us from your hand, O king."

Isn't their response just incredible? This is the exact response all Christians should have when we are asked to do something that deters us from worshiping our Almighty God. We need to remember that it's not our job to defend ourselves. Scripture reminds us that God is our defender (Proverbs 23:11). Shadrach, Meshach and Abednego trusted that God was able to save them from the fiery furnace. Though they didn't know if God would choose to save them physically, they trusted that God would save them spiritually. The men were also confident to say, "But even if he does not, we want you to know, O king, that we will not serve your gods or worship the image of gold you have set up." What a bold and profound statement. Oh, to trust God the way these faithful men did!

As many of us know, the Lord spared the lives of these three men after allowing them to be thrown into the fiery furnace that was heated up seven times hotter than usual. But despite the tremendous heat, no harm had been done to their bodies, and not a single hair on their heads was singed. The smell of smoke couldn't even be detected on them. This should make us all stand in awe of our God who saves.

In sheer amazement of the unharmed men, King Nebuchadnezzar called for them to come out and said, "Praise be to the God of Shadrach, Meshach and Abednego, who has sent his angel and rescued his servants!" King Nebuchadnezzar went on to proclaim what these three courageous men did while they waited upon the Lord to be rescued. He said, "They trusted in him and defied the king's command and were willing to give up their lives rather than serve or worship any god except their own God."

The word *trust* brings to my mind the old hymn entitled, "Trust and Obey." Verse three says:

"But we never can prove the delights of His love until all on the altar we lay;
For the favor He shows, for the joy He bestows,
are for them who will trust and obey."

"Until *all* on the altar we lay." Wow! Those are profound words. God's favor is granted to those who will trust in Him alone, despite whatever human sacrifice may be required. For Shadrach, Meshach and Abednego, this meant their physical lives were at stake. Yet they valued their spiritual lives so much more and were willing to lose it all for the sake of Christ. What a testimony!

I'm impacted by the lessons that can be learned from these three faithful men who put their trust in God while they waited upon the Lord's deliverance on their lives:

- They stood unified as brothers in Christ

- They trusted fully in their Sovereign God

- They were willing to sacrifice their physical lives in order to worship God alone

Based on their testimony of faith and the Sovereignty of God, even King Nebuchadnezzar had to admit to all the people in the nation that, "No other god can save in this way." Praise the Lord! No one else could have stated that better. There is no god, except the Almighty God Himself, who is mighty to save.

EVEN IF

One of my favorite Christian songs on the radio right now is *"Even If"* by MercyMe. The lyrics in the first verse remind us that it's easy to trust God when life is going our way. But we have a choice to make when life gets hard. The challenge is this ... will we still trust God when life doesn't go our way?

The lyrics to the chorus of this song say:

> *I know You're able and I know You can*
>
> *Save through the fire with Your mighty hand*
>
> *But even if You don't*
>
> *My hope is You alone*

In the second verse of this song, we're reminded that God may choose to leave some mountains unmovable in our lives. For example, what if you've faithfully prayed for physical healing but end up getting diagnosed with a terminal illness? What if your marriage falls apart? What if you lose your job and have to use up your hard-earned savings to survive financially? The what-if's of life are endless. This song challenges us to depend upon the Lord to give us His strength so we can continue to sing, *"It is well with my soul,"* through those difficult times. As Psalm 57:7 states, "My heart is steadfast, O God, my heart is steadfast; I will sing and make music." This needs to be our heart's response regardless of the situations we face. With God, it can be well with our souls—always.

That type of a response isn't easy, but it's necessary. It's not our first choice, but it's the godly choice. Consider whatever it might be that you're waiting for right now. It's natural for each one of us to have hopes, dreams and desired outcomes while we anticipate our waiting periods to come to an end. But what if God's outcomes don't match up with ours? What will we do then? How will we respond? We must remind ourselves that *even if* God doesn't choose to answer our prayers in the way we desire, it can still be well with our souls because our hope solely rests in the fact that He is in control and He is mighty to save.

MARY AND JONAH—CHALLENGED TO TRUST GOD

Earlier in the book, we referenced Mary's response to the angel Gabriel when she was told she would bear God's Son, Jesus. Her reply was, "I am your servant. May it be to me as you have said."

Though Mary's first question to the angel was, "How will this be since I am a virgin?" she wasn't doubting the truth of God's sovereign plan. Notice that she didn't question the angel by saying, "How can this be?" she remarked, "How will this be?" There's a big difference between the two words *can* and *will*. The word *can* expresses doubt and uncertainty where the word *will* demonstrates belief with curiosity. The angel reminded Mary in Luke 1:37 that, "Nothing is impossible with God," and that's exactly what Mary chose to focus on. Though she was very aware that conceiving a baby as a virgin was humanly impossible, she was reminded that conceiving a baby as a virgin through God was possible.

Jonah is another example for us in the Bible who was challenged to trust God. However, unlike Mary who submitted immediately to the Lord's calling for her to bear His Son, Jesus, it's interesting to note that Jonah's verbal alignment with God happened after he ran from the Lord's command.

God said this to Jonah, "Go to the great city of Nineveh and preach against it, because its wickedness has come up before me." What was Jonah's response to the Lord's command? He ran away. He went aboard a ship headed for Tarshish to flee from the Lord" (see Jonah 1:1-3). Sounds kind of crazy, right? But how many times does that happen to us? We hear a word from the Lord, or we know the calling He's placed on our hearts, and our immediate reaction is to run rather than submit.

Many times, we get scared when we hear God's voice because He may be asking us to do something undesirable, or something impossible.

However, looking back at what we learned from Mary, we are reminded by the angel's words that, "Nothing is impossible with God" (Luke 1:37). Jonah didn't trust God the way Mary did. He was consumed by frustration and insecurity. I'm guessing that Mary may have been struck with some human insecurities, just like Jonah, but she chose to have greater faith in God than in her circumstances. Where Mary clung to trust, Jonah clung to rebellion. Oh, how we could all benefit by growing our trust in the Lord more and more.

What trial or difficulty are you faced with right now? What impossibility is staring you right between the eyes? Are you at a roadblock where you feel completely hopeless? If so, then ask yourself, are you going through this situation alone, or are you going through it with God? You see friends, there *is* hope with God, but we are hopeless on our own. There *is* strength with God, yet we are powerless on our own. There *is* peace that passes all understanding with God, yet we are helpless on our own. As Jesus shared with his disciples multiple times, "With man this is impossible, but with God all things are possible" (Matthew 19:26). Rest in the endless possibilities that come from living a life with God.

TRUSTING BASED UPON KNOWING

We can trust someone to the point that we know them. If that's true, how well would you say you are trusting God right now? If you're having trouble answering that question then ask yourself, "How well do I know God?" It's one thing to know *about* God, but how well do you personally *know* Him? Getting to know someone takes time and effort. We need to sacrifice things in order to carve out time to spend with God, and we need to have a desire to know Him deeper than we know Him right now. No one can fathom the depths of God, yet we need to encourage one another to keep growing in Him.

We need to caution ourselves from maintaining a surface relationship with our all-powerful, all-knowing, all-sufficient God. Don't be satisfied with a little bit of God. Don't desire just some of Him. Desire to know God to the fullest extent that He is willing to reveal Himself to you.

Just as the strongest trees have the deepest roots, that's how we are to be rooted in Christ. That's why God tells us in Scripture that those He finds favor with may be called "oaks of righteousness" (Isaiah 61:3). When we are deeply rooted in God, we are rooted in His unfathomable depths. We don't need to understand His depths, we simply need to keep growing in them.

God is faithful. We can be certain that He will hold to His promises. We never have to question or doubt. If we truly believe God is good, then we can leave everything at His disposal ... our hopes, our dreams and our desires. We can rest assured that if He does not give us the human comforts we desire, He will grant us His wiser determinations. It might not feel like an uncomfortable situation is best for our lives, but we must choose to live this life based upon what we *know* about God, rather than what we *feel* about a situation. He is good ... all the time. Our walk with God must be solely based on facts rather than feelings. Regardless of our circumstances, we must know that God, as Arthur G. Bennett wrote in *The Valley of Vision*, is a "bottomless fountain of all good."

How can we know that we're trusting in God? The answer is revealed to us in Romans 15:13 where it says, "May the God of hope, fill you with all joy and peace as you trust in him, so that you may overflow with hope by the power of the Holy Spirit." Joy and peace are the direct result of trusting in Him. Though we can be surrounded by difficulties, trials and tribulations, we can simultaneously rest in the joy and peace that passes all understanding as we trust in God. We bear the fruit of the Spirit when we trust in Him. God produces the fruit in our lives. Our job is to bear it. We're also reminded in the book of Nehemiah that, "the joy of the LORD is [our] strength" (Nehemiah 8:10). So, if we put both of these thoughts together, what does it look like?

Trust → Joy and Peace → STRENGTH

At times, I wish there was a formula to simplify this Christian life. I'd love a textbook to show me spiritually where A+B=C. That just seems to make sense to me from all of the algebra classes I took years ago. But God doesn't demonstrate Himself to us according to a formula. He reveals Himself to us through faith.

$$Trust + Obedience \rightarrow FAITH$$

There's freedom when we live by faith and living by faith is what pleases God.

CAST YOUR CARES

It may be easy for many of us to say that we're trusting God while we wait for His leading on our lives, but it's quite another thing to demonstrate our faith while we wait. So how do we do that? What happens when the weight of our wait becomes too heavy of a load to bear and it overwhelms us?

Though it can be a little unnerving at times, there truly is freedom when we live by faith. And we must remember that faith is what pleases God. Oh, that we would respond to the Lord just as the apostles did years ago when they said, "Increase our faith!" The amazing part of faith is what God promised to us in Matthew 17:20 when He said, "If you have faith as small as a mustard seed, you can say to this mountain, 'Move from here to there, and it will move. Nothing will be impossible for you.'" Isn't that an incredible thought? The tiniest bit of genuine faith in God can make anything possible. Now that's overwhelming!

Many people are familiar with the verse found in 1 Peter 5:7 that says, "Cast all your anxiety on him because he cares for you." Though we know what the words of that verse say, have we really meditated on what those words mean? Personally, I find it very easy to recite the words, but I find it very difficult at times to implement them. Why is it so hard for me to cast all my anxiety on the Lord? Why wouldn't I be eager to give Him all of my burdens? Could it be that I really don't trust Him the way I think I do?

Let's look at the idea of casting our cares onto the Lord in greater detail by using an example. Imagine for a moment that you're an employee at a professional business. What would you do if you had a co-worker who caused great difficulty or frustration for you on the job each day? Depending on your personality, as well as your specific circumstances, you may choose to brush it off and let it go. But in other instances, you may choose to quit your job altogether. Those are the two extremes to this situation.

However, there's another possibility. If you desired to keep working at your job, but conflict persisted and began to affect your working environment in an extremely negative way, you may have to take your issue *(care)* to an individual having more authority than you in order to have it dealt with in a professional and appropriate manner (i.e. a manager, boss, Human Resource personnel, etc.). When you take your complaint or concern to a person who has greater authority and influence than you, you are *"casting your care"* onto that individual. In reality, once you share your issue with that person, you're asking them to handle it for you. You no longer choose to stay in control of the situation. Even though you may be slightly bothered by it from time to time, you trust that it is being handled by someone who can, and will, assist in reconciling the situation for you. You choose to let it go, rather than keep clinging to it.

This is how it's meant to be between us and God. When we struggle with hardships or difficulties in this world, God doesn't want us to carry those burdens by ourselves. He wants us to lighten our load by casting our cares onto Him so we can be relieved of life's burdens that tend to weigh us down. God wants us to depend on Him as our number one source of authority who can, and will, meet our every need. He wants us to exchange our heavy burdens for His light yoke. That's why Jesus died on the cross for us. He took on the sin of this entire world so He could offer us a life of spiritual freedom. He doesn't want His children weighed down by the things of this world. We receive rest for our souls when we're willing to surrender our weighted burdens onto Him (Matthew 11:28-30). Lighten your load and entrust Him, dear friends, with whatever it is that you're waiting for. Release the weight of your wait onto Him.

Though that may sound simple, why is it so hard for us to do? It really comes down to the idea of control. Our human nature craves to be in the driver's seat of our lives. We like to know where we're going, determine how we're going to get there, and plan the end result. But the idea of trust means that we agree to give control to someone else … namely, God. Trust means we're willing to surrender to the direction, path and outcome of God's plan for our lives, rather than carry out our own plans. That can be both intimidating and uncomfortable for us.

Though trusting God can make us feel uneasy at times, we must believe that God's ways and thoughts are not like ours. They are always better (Isaiah 55:8-9). As a matter of fact, they aren't just *better*, they are the *best*. How is that possible? Because He's perfect. God is only capable of giving us His best all the time, nothing less. Isn't that both comforting and amazing?

We must also keep in mind that God's plans and purposes are always meant to prosper us and not harm us. His plans promise to give us hope and a future (Jeremiah 29:11). The question becomes this: Do we really believe these verses are true? The struggle many of us may have is that we believe these words about God are true, but we don't necessarily have a confidence that confirms what those words say. Dear friends, may we be reminded that our faith is based merely on the *facts* of God's and not on our *feelings*. God's Word is truth and our security needs to rest in the words of His truth alone.

God doesn't only demonstrate His graciousness to us by being willing to take our burdens away. He also demonstrates His compassion to us by offering us two amazing gifts when we place our trust in Him. As we referenced a little earlier, the benefits of trusting God are joy and peace. Isn't that comforting? God not only wants to relieve us from our heavy burdens, He also wants to entrust us with the gift of fruit that comes from the Holy Spirit. Romans 15:13 says, "May the God of hope fill you with all joy and peace as you trust in him, so that you may overflow with hope by the power of the Holy Spirit."

As you wait upon the Lord, trust Him enough to cast your burdens onto Him so you can experience His joy and peace that passes all understanding. Live freely from the weight of your wait as you enjoy the fruit of joy and peace.

Trusting God More than Circumstances

By placing our trust in God, we release our control of situations and circumstances over to God. We can be free from added responsibility that was never intended for us to have in the first place. We experience freedom in Christ rather than bondage.

Let's consider a man who's referenced in the Bible in the book of John (John 4:46-53). This man was a royal government official who had a very sick son. When the man heard that Jesus was in town, he went to Him and begged Jesus to come heal his son who was near the point of death. The royal official said, "Sir, come down before my child dies." But Jesus replied, "You may go. Your son will live."

The next line of verse 50 is what delights my heart. It says, "The man took Jesus at his word and departed." You see, we all crave to see Jesus work His miracles. Living by sight is what gives us the most comfort in this world. Most of us can relate to the phrase, "Seeing is believing." But that's not what faith is. This official understood that faith was simply taking God at His word, regardless if He ever saw God perform the miracle in front of him or not. He walked away with his heart filled with the promise of Jesus' words, "Your son will live." And while the man was still walking home, his servants met him with the news that his boy was living. This man simply trusted in the words of the Miracle Maker rather than the act of the miracle itself. Oh, that we would have that same kind of faith!

The truth of the matter is that we *can* have this same type of faith. We have the same opportunity to believe in the words and promises of Jesus, just like this royal official did. Proverbs 3:5-6 says,

Trust in the Lord with all your heart and lean not on your own understanding; in all your ways acknowledge him and he will make your paths straight.

If we truly want to have faith in God, the very first thing we need to do is place our full trust in Him. God says we need to give Him *all* of our heart ... not just some of it. That doesn't mean we simply give God our circumstances and our hopeful outcomes. It's far greater than that. Giving God all of our heart means that we give Him ourselves. It means that we're willing to surrender our inmost being to Him. We give Him our soul and spirit to do as He pleases, and what pleases Him is to ultimately glorify Himself through us. We commit to letting God rule over our hearts and lives. We agree to let Him be our Lord and Savior. Not because we have to, but because we want to.

You see, life is a choice. Not a single one of us had the choice to be born into this world physically. As a matter of fact, if we knew what this sinful world was all about before the day of our birth, I bet many of us would have chosen not to enter it. We entered this world because someone else made that choice for us ... whether it was planned or not. But even though we didn't get to choose our physical life, each one of us has been given the opportunity to choose our spiritual life ... our eternal destiny.

We live in a world that craves choices. We want things done our way and within our preferred time frames. Fast food restaurants have grasped an exceptional understanding of this idea by creating advertisements that promote the ideas of "Have it your way!" and "You deserve a break today!" The subliminal message being conveyed to the customer is, "We understand your wants and needs. We want you to be happy. Choose us to be satisfied!"

Package delivery services provide satisfaction to our timely demands by promising "on-time, every time" deliveries. Businesses crave repeat customers so many of them are now willing to provide 100 percent satisfaction guarantees on their goods and services. With so many options to choose from, which one will we pick to satisfy our greatest need in any particular situation? Sometimes there are so many choices that the decision-making process can be overwhelming.

God understands our desire for choices far better than profitable businesses do. But His primary concern is regarding the choices we make in terms of our spiritual lives. God understands our spiritual needs so well that He demonstrated the most selfless decision that ever has, and ever will be, recorded in history. Let me explain ...

You see, back in Genesis 3, human beings chose to allow sin to enter the world. God didn't desire that for us, but He selflessly gave us the gift of free will. Unfortunately, we chose sin over righteousness. When Adam and Eve ate of the forbidden fruit in the Garden of Eden, we were immediately separated from God.

Now you might be uncomfortable with the fact that I used the word *we* in the previous sentences. Wasn't this incident tied directly to Adam and Eve? It most certainly was. However, Adam and Eve simply represented the human race then, as we represent it now. They had the opportunity to continue living in a perfect earthly paradise as long as they didn't eat of the fruit God prohibited of them in the middle of the garden. So, what went wrong? It came down to their need to make a choice. They were tempted by the crafty serpent when he said to the woman, "You will not surely die, for God knows that when you eat of it your eyes will be opened and you will be like God, knowing good and evil" (vs 4-5).

What happened next was the first choice that changed paradise as they knew it. Eve took some of the fruit and ate it. She then gave some of the fruit to Adam who ate of it as well (vs 6). Though eating the forbidden fruit was the outward act that brought sin into this world, there's a key point that I don't want us to miss in verse five that led up to this turning point.

Adam and Eve already knew that they would surely die if they ate from the tree of the knowledge of good and evil because God had told them so (Genesis 2:17; Genesis 3:3). They initially trusted God's word as being accurate and true. They didn't question, refute or argue with the Lord when He set up that boundary. They accepted and held fast to what

God impressed upon them in paradise until temptation crept in with an option to choose a different way.

Trust was broken and doubt set in when temptation himself (Satan) approached Eve with an alternative that appeared better than the perfect life they were already experiencing. Satan enticed Eve with the thought that her eyes would be open and she would become like God, knowing good and evil (Genesis 3:5). Up to that point, Adam and Eve had trusted God to guide them in the way of good and evil, but their trust in God was being put to the ultimate test. Would they continue trusting in God's perfect plans, or would they be better off believing they could become like God by simply choosing a different way?

Now let's pause here for a moment and quickly define what trust is. When we trust someone, or something, we have full confidence in that person or thing. Another word for trust is faith. God clearly explains what faith is in Hebrews 11:1 which says, "Now faith is being sure of what we hope for and certain of what we do not see." Did you catch the last several words of that verse? A key component to faith is being certain of *what we do not see*. That's a hard concept for us to grasp. It goes against nearly everything this world is teaching us. We like to know things before we commit to them. We want facts so we're not caught off-guard or blindsided. We desire proof to be certain that we're not making a big mistake. After all, our insecurities can get the best of us. But true faith is trusting in what we cannot see. Having faith can be a little scary. It can feel a bit risky. But it's necessary in order for us to have a relationship with Jesus Christ that will result in a perfect heavenly paradise, like the paradise God gifted to Adam and Eve on earth before they chose to break their trust with God.

You see, the real danger wasn't lurking when Satan approached Eve, tempting her with an alternative to God's plan for their lives. He was simply a decoy that could have been avoided by Eve's willingness to continue trusting God, submitting to Him as she already had been up to that point. All she had to do was, "resist the devil, and he [would] flee" (James 4:7). But instead of keeping her eyes and mind fixed on God, she saw that the fruit of the tree was good for food, pleasing to the eye, and also desirable for gaining wisdom (Genesis 3:6) ... so she took the first bite of sin.

Isn't that the same way for us? We live in a world chock-full of temptation. I personally think that temptation can be the strongest in our lives when we experience periods of waiting. If we don't keep our eyes and minds focused on God while we wait, we will have a hard time—actually, an impossible time—resisting the devil, just like Eve. If we allow our *waits* to become *weights* in our lives, we'll quickly learn that the burdens we choose to carry are far too difficult for us to bear. As the burdens get heavy, so does the temptation for us to gravitate toward quick, and potentially dangerous, decisions. We'll find ourselves seeking nearly any alternative that looks "good, pleasing and desirable" to our naked eyes, just like Eve.

Eve craved the forbidden fruit more than she craved obeying God in that particular moment of time. She fell victim to the words of temptation that came her way. She considered the fruit to be good and pleasing, or she wouldn't have chosen it. In a moment of weakness, Eve desired the physical over the spiritual. Her moment of earthly pleasure resulted in a lack of trust in God. The consequence was guilt and shame. The consequence was sin.

Referring back to Proverbs 3:5, we are commanded by God to trust in Him alone for our salvation as well as for our daily needs. He is our Protector and Provider. We are not to trust in the things of this world, which are only temporal and physical. We are to trust in Him. He is spiritual and eternal. His is our hope of everlasting life through the shed blood of Jesus Christ. That's all ... nothing else.

God has fulfilled every promise in Scripture. Trust Him. His Word is truth (John 17:17). Trust Him. He is faithful. Trust Him. He is our Redeemer, Savior and Friend. Trust Him. He is our only hope. Trust Him with your life ... both now and forever. He is our salvation. Trust only in Him, dear friends, and claim these familiar hymnal words as your very own:

My hope is built on nothing less than Jesus blood and righteousness, I dare not trust the sweetest frame, but wholly lean on Jesus Name. On Christ the Solid Rock I stand, all other ground is sinking sand, all other ground is sinking sand.

We need to trust God with all of our heart, not just some of it. God's not interested in us just trusting Him with the daily issues we face. Sure, He wants us to trust Him with those, but He's most concerned about us first devoting our hearts to Him. He wants us to surrender *ourselves* before we surrender our issues. He wants our spirit and soul to follow Him. He wants us to make an eternal commitment to follow Him. We can get so consumed with the "here and now" that we lose sight of the forever and ever. Give Him your all, dear ones. Give Him your heart.

Each one of us is in need of a Savior. Scripture reminds us that, "All have sinned and fall short of the glory of God" (Romans 3:23). Did you catch that? *All* have sinned, which means each one of us have fallen short of God's glory. We are all destined for hell. But God, through His grace and mercy, made a way for us to be able to inherit the Kingdom of God despite our sin. "While we were sinners, Christ died for us" (Romans 5:8).

If you haven't already done so, admit that you are a sinner in need of a Savior. Make this a defining moment in your life. Pray to the Lord. Ask Jesus to forgive you and invite Him into your heart so He can reign over your life, over your decisions, and over your weights. God promises us in John 1:12, "Yet to all who received him, to those who believed in his name, he gave the right to become children of God." We have the opportunity to choose Christ. If you've just done that, I welcome you into the family of God! Now that you've trusted God with your heart, you can start trusting Him with you circumstances. Keep your mind fixed on God and continue trusting in the One you cannot yet see. Let Him grow your faith. One day He will be revealed to you and me ... oh what a glorious day that will be!

DISCUSSION QUESTIONS:

1. Just like David, we are expected to wait upon the Lord until we learn what God will do for us in different situations.

   a. Do you wait patiently after inquiring of the Lord, knowing that He hears, He sees and He answers? Explain.

   _____

   _____

   _____

   _____

   b. Do you rush into decisions before consulting God and waiting for His response? Why or why not?

   _____

   _____

   _____

   _____

2. What are some practical ways you could improve the way you wait upon the Lord?

   _____

   _____

   _____

   _____

3. It's pretty easy to trust God when life is going our way, but what happens when life gets hard? What if God's outcomes don't match up with yours? How will you prepare yourself to respond in a godly way?

   _____

   _____

   _____

   _____

4. Think about how you typically respond when God asks you to do something difficult or uncomfortable.

    a. What types of situations cause you to run away like Jonah?

_____

_____

_____

_____

    b. When are you most likely to embrace difficult situations, remembering that you are a servant of the Lord like Mary?

_____

_____

_____

_____

5. How well would you say you know God? Do you know *about* Him or do you truly *know* Him? Explain.

_____

_____

_____

_____

6. In general, is it easy or difficult for you to cast your cares upon the Lord? Share your thoughts.

_____

_____

_____

_____

7. Do you truly believe God's plans are to give you hope and a future rather than harm you? Explain.

_____

_____

_____

_____

8. What is one of your greatest temptations in life and how do you try to overcome it?

_____

_____

_____

_____

GROW IN GOD'S GRACE

Second Peter 3:17 says that while we wait for the Lord's return, we must caution ourselves from being "carried away by the error of lawless men" so we don't "fall from [our] secure position." So, what should we do instead of being carried away by lawless men? We must "grow in the grace and knowledge of our Lord and Savior Jesus Christ" (vs 18).

Growth seems natural, right? Babies born without defect naturally grow from an infant to a child to a teen to an adult. Spiritually, our growth process should take place in the same way. Scripture defines a person's spiritual growth stages as being that of an infant who grows into a child then into a young man and, ultimately, into a father. However, this process is supernatural. There is nothing natural about an individual's spiritual growth. Spiritual growth requires the intervention, and transformation, by God Himself. Remember what John 15:5b says, "Apart from me, you can do nothing." Nothing! We can't grow without God. We will remain mere spiritual infants if we don't cling to, and depend upon, God for growth. It is only through the power of the Holy Spirit that we will mature in our faith walk with God.

We need to have a burning desire stirred up in our hearts in order to grow spiritually. That requires passion and effort, unlike our physical beings. Again, spiritual growth requires God. Physically, we need food and water to grow. Spiritually, we need food (God's Word), water (Jesus—the Living Water; the person of Christ) and application (God's

Word being lived out through us). We need to put into practice the things we learn from God. This is a key concept to becoming more like Christ, living out what we truly believe. If we don't take a step of faith to support the food and water that has filled us, our heads will continue to grow with knowledge but our hearts will not develop at the same pace. We will become spiritual "bobble-heads." And that's not a look any of us Christians want to have! The goal is for our minds and hearts to develop in sync with each another. We need to practice living out what we're learning while we're learning it.

As we grow physically, our bodies stretch to new lengths. Based on the rate of our physical growth, some people actually experience growing pains. Depending on the speed of growth, growing pains can become extremely uncomfortable. Whether we grow physically, emotionally or spiritually, we must remember that growth is a process. It takes time. It can be uncomfortable and difficult to bear. But the result is typically bigger, wiser, and stronger. No pain, no gain.

Let's consider the word *stretch* for a minute. In Matthew 12:9-14, Jesus had gone into a synagogue. A man with a shriveled hand was there. Jesus told the man to stretch out his hand. The man obeyed Him and his hand was completely restored.

Though we're not given any other details from this story about the process of the man's healing, I can't help but wonder if the process of completely stretching out his hand from a shriveled state hurt him at all. I mean, think about it. If you've ever dealt with arthritis, joint pain, or have simply had your hand fall asleep, it can hurt as you try to stretch it out.

Sometimes we'd rather live with our existing pain rather than go through the pain that can result from the healing process. All we know from this story is that God told the man to stretch out his hand. The man immediately obeyed and his hand was restored. The man trusted in the grace of God and he was healed. Remarkable!

Looking back at 2 Peter 3:18, we are told that, "We must grow in the grace and knowledge of our Lord and Savior Jesus Christ." Notice that we're told we *must grow*. As children of God, spiritual growth is not an option. A follower of Christ should sense both a responsibility and a desire to continually grow in the Lord. We must caution ourselves from becoming stagnant or complacent in our Christian lives. Complacency represents a decaying faith. Growth represents a faith that is flourishing. A flourishing faith is one that testifies of Christ.

In that same verse we're also told that, "We must grow *in the grace and knowledge of our Lord and Savior Jesus Christ.*" It's not that we should grow in grace *or* knowledge. We must grow in both. The only way we can grow in the grace of Christ is to grow in our knowledge of Christ. Our goal needs to be like the apostle Paul as he shared in Philippians 3:10 when he said, "I want to know Christ and the power of his resurrection and the fellowship of sharing in his sufferings, becoming like him in his death." Once we understand who Christ is, what He did for us by dying on the cross for our sins, and how He rose again to be with God the Father in Heaven, only then do we start understanding the gift of grace.

We must understand that grace is receiving something we never earned or deserved. We must understand that grace is a free gift. By understanding grace, we can appreciate how we've been given the opportunity to receive Jesus Christ as our personal Lord and Savior. We have the opportunity to claim Him as our Master, our Lord and Savior. We can choose to give Him control of our lives while we rest in His loving arms. We don't deserve His grace, but we are given the opportunity to receive it and extend it to others. The more we choose to know Him, the more we'll desire to grow in Him.

Let's reflect back on Mary, the mother of Jesus. As was mentioned earlier, when Mary was told by the angel Gabriel that she'd give birth to God's Son, her response was, "How will this be since I am a virgin?" She could've said, "How *can* this be?" By responding with the word *will*, Mary was demonstrating her spiritual maturity as a young teenage girl. She responded with grace. She knew that all things were possible with God, and she was willing to let God show her how it would all come to fruition.

Now, let's be clear. Mary's response doesn't mean she wasn't a bit overwhelmed, slightly scared, or didn't have a million questions racing through her head. However, those details aren't revealed to us in Scripture, so we can only interpret what has been shared.

What we can infer is that Mary was being stretched by God then, just like we are being stretched by Him now. Mary was simply willing to trust God to grow her faith and grace through that specific situation. She would have to wait nine months to see the physical proof from God that, indeed, the Messiah would be born from her virgin body. God grew Mary spiritually as He stretched her both physically and emotionally throughout her pregnancy. Her graceful response pleased the Lord when she replied, "I am the Lord's servant. May it be to me as you have said."

Many times, our humanness wants to flip that response and tell God, "May it be to me as *I* have said." But that's not the response of a true follower of God. We humanly crave for our will to be done, but a godly heart prays for the will of God to be done through us. Mary's response was one of obedience. Now that's a heart that is rooted both in the grace and faith of God.

As you wait upon the Lord's direction for your life, are you willing to respond in the same way as Mary did, regardless of what He may ask of you? What if His request is far different than your expectations might be? What if He calls you to do something that's completely out of your comfort zone? Are you still willing to walk in obedience remembering that you are the Lord's servant? Are you willing to do whatever He says?

In Acts 4 we're challenged by the way believers in Jesus' day grew in grace based on what they did with their possessions. In verses 32-35, we're told that they had one heart and mind. They took no ownership of their own possessions. They shared everything they had. The apostles continued testifying of the Lord Jesus Christ. During that time, there was no needy person among them because God's grace was at work in them all. Everything they had and did was for the benefit of their group.

As I think of that period of time, I wonder how many of those believers had hopes and dreams of their own. I wonder how many of them were waiting for a specific direction in their lives that was different than the one they were living out. I wonder how many of them thought, "Is this it God? Is this what You've called us to do?" Despite whatever they may have personally been thinking, they used that time to love one another. They extended grace to each other by sharing everything they had. They humbled themselves by not taking ownership of anything the Lord had given them. It says that God's grace was powerfully at work in them. Obviously, God's grace was growing them.

Then in Acts 20:22-24, it references the time when Paul was directed by the Spirit to go to Jerusalem. He admitted to the Ephesian elders that he didn't know what would happen to him there. He had to wait for the Lord to reveal that to him. The only thing he knew for sure was that prison and hardship awaited him in every city where the Holy Spirit had previously led him. And if the Spirit was the one leading him now to Jerusalem, he was quite certain that prison awaited him there as well. Even with that reality in mind, Paul was adamant that he considered his life to be nothing for himself. He simply wanted to finish the race God set before him and complete the task of testifying to the good news of God's grace.

Paul wasn't going to stop proclaiming God's grace no matter what hardships stood in his way. As we share God's grace, we grow in God's grace. If you're in a waiting period right now, uncertain of what awaits you, are you willing to testify of the good news of God's grace while you wait? Reflect for a minute and ask yourself, "Who does God have in my life right now? What opportunities does God have in front of me where I can share the love of Christ with others?"

Isaiah 26:8-9 says, "Yes, Lord, walking in the way of your laws, we wait [long] for you; your name and renown are the desire of our hearts. My soul yearns for you in the night; in the morning my spirit longs for you …"

I find it so interesting that the word *walk* and *wait* are used in the same verse. Many times, we struggle as Christians wondering what we should be doing while we wait upon the Lord for an answer. But then we come across a verse like this that tells us exactly what we should be doing. Our job is to walk in the ways of God while we wait upon Him. We'll know we're walking with God when we find ourselves being obedient to His Word. We'll know we're walking with God when the name and fame of God consumes our minds more than the answer to whatever it is that we're waiting for. When we long for God more than the things of this world, we're walking with Him and are becoming the people of grace that He has always intended us to be. Men and woman of grace look to the God of grace so they can be filled abundantly by His grace while they wait.

Sometimes I get so caught up in the thought of *what* a person of grace looks like that I lose sight of *whom* they look to while they wait. A person of grace looks to the God of grace. Is the name and renown of God the sole desire of our hearts? I don't want these verses to just be my prayer. I want them to be my life. Grow me in Your grace, O Lord!

In many ways, I believe this Christian walk is simpler than we tend to make it. There is not a degree, line or level, to determine how much of something we are in Christ. We are *all* or *nothing* based upon whether or not we have a personal relationship with Jesus. God has given us life abundantly in Christ. The fullness of Him is in us if we are saved. We complicate things when we try to decide how holy, graceful, righteous, selfish or sinful we are.

We have the opportunity to delight in God's grace each and every day. How are you and I doing with that? If we're delighting in God's grace, then the result will be obedience. How can this be? It's simple. We can't act on sin and delight in God's grace at the same time. According to Romans 6, we can't go on sinning while grace abounds. Since we have been freed from the bondage of sin through the death, burial and resurrection of Jesus Christ, the barriers between ourselves and God have been removed. The result is that we may now choose to stop sinning in order to delight in God's grace (Romans 6:18). Think of that for a moment. The fullness of God's grace resides in you. Now ask yourself, if you have the choice to obey God or sin against Him while you wait, and you know that the fullness of His grace is in you, which choice will you make? We know the choice we *should* make, but is it the choice we *will* make?

Since each believer has received the fullness of God's grace upon becoming saved, why does it appear that some Christians have more of His grace than others? Let me share an example using the illustration of a flower. Let's choose a tulip.

Imagine that you're going to plant a bunch of tulip bulbs in your yard. Each bulb contains everything it needs in order to develop and grow into a fully bloomed flower over time. Spiritually speaking, let's say that each bulb represents the fullness of God's grace given to each believer. Once a person becomes saved, the tulip bulb (God's grace) is planted deep within each believer's heart. All believers receive the same amount of God's grace the moment they become saved. No one gets more or less than another. Keep in mind that the *whole* bulb is planted immediately upon a person's spiritual conversion, not just part of it. The fullness of God's grace resides in each believer and the Holy Spirit is readily at work as He teaches, nourishes and guides each one as they choose to walk with God.

In the spring of each year, I walk out to the back of my house to look at the progressive growth of each flower. Some of them are beginning to pop up along the back side of my house where the sun shines brightest. The progression of their growth is exciting to see as their stems rise high. As the flower petals begin opening, the heart of the tulip is revealed. However, as I scan the area further, I can see that there are other tulips that grew up out of the ground, but their petals remain closed. I can see the evidence of their external color but I can't enjoy the full beauty that remains inside because their petals remain closed. Though there is still beauty in the coloring of a closed tulip, it's not the same beauty as one that is fully blossomed.

Just like actual flowers, some believers will bud, while others will fully bloom. However, regardless of the result, we must remember that the potential for each flower to fully blossom is in each bulb. That's the same concept regarding God's grace planted in each believer. The fullness of God's grace lies within each individual who has committed to trust in Jesus Christ as his or her personal Lord and Savior. But not all of us will experience the fullness of God's grace if we don't continue to grow and flourish in Him. Others may know that we're saved by God's grace, but they may never experience God's grace through us if we only bud, and not fully bloom, in our relationship with Him.

God's grace doesn't automatically grow in us chronologically as we age. The display of His grace depends on our desperate desire to grow in Him. Grace develops and reveals itself in us as we grow in our longing for God. The more dependent upon Him we are, the more His grace shines through us. Grace is extended to the degree that believers are willing to listen to, and obey, the calling that the Lord places on our hearts. Our job is not hard. We are simply called to bloom where we've been planted.

Maybe you've been planted in a painful season of life where you find yourself just waiting right now. You may be lacking answers that you desperately crave and may be feeling very alone. Your season may feel like a burden much more than a blessing. Know that God sees you and is growing you right where you are. He has not abandoned or forsaken you. He cares for you deeply and He is with you. He is the gardener tending to your every need while you wait. He is using this time and place to grow you into the likeness of Himself. He is using this time of wait to reveal His grace through you. Rather than stay closed up and discouraged, choose to blossom and let His grace abound in you. Be willing to bloom where you've been planted.

DISCUSSION QUESTIONS:

1. What have you been learning from God lately and how have you been actively living that out?

   _____

   _____

   _____

   _____

2. Are you in a difficult season of waiting right now? If so, how are you responding to God as you walk through it?

   _____

   _____

   _____

   _____

3. Consider Mary's response to the angel when she was told she would give birth to God's son, Jesus. She said, *"I am the Lord's servant. May it be to me as you have said"* (Luke 1:38). Regardless of what God may ask of you, are you willing to respond in a similar way? Consider the following questions and share your thoughts.

   > What if God's request is far different than your expectations might be? What if He calls you to do something that's completely out of your comfort zone? Are you still willing to walk in obedience remembering that you are the Lord's servant? Are you willing to do whatever He says?

   _____

   _____

   _____

   _____

4. Even if you're experiencing a difficult season of life right now, are you willing to testify of the good news of God's grace while you walk through it? If so, how? If not, why?

_____

_____

_____

_____

5. Take a moment and ask yourself, *"Who does God have in my life right now? What opportunities does God have in front of me where I can share the love of Christ with others?"* Share your thoughts.

_____

_____

_____

_____

6. We have the opportunity to delight in God's grace each and every day. How are you doing with that? If you're struggling to delight is His grace, what could you do to change that?

_____

_____

_____

_____

7. Considering the illustration of a tulip, how would you describe how you've been growing in God's grace? Do you see yourself as a closed bulb, or are you blossoming more and more? Explain.

_____

_____

_____

_____

8

BE TRANSFORMED

IN THE BOOK *BECOMING A Woman Whose God is Enough,* Cynthia Heald makes some interesting points regarding the fact that God isn't obligated to meet our personal wants or desires. She states that, "The Lord has our best interest at heart when He denies us what we think we need." Stop and think about that for a moment. What thoughts come to mind when you consider that statement? Do we really believe that God has our best interest at heart when He denies us what we think we need? Does God really know what we need more than we do? How can the denial of a want or need be in our best interest when the pain of not receiving it can be so great?

As I've pondered these thoughts, I can't help but think of the words in Jeremiah 17:9 that say, "The heart is deceitful above all things and beyond cure. Who can understand it?" We *think* we know what's best for us, but God *knows* what's best for us. We think we have a clear conscience, pure thoughts and right motives, but only God knows our heart. It's not that we never have right intentions or motives for desiring certain things, but we can deceive ourselves. If we're not careful, we can be easily swayed by the people and situations around us. What we think may be best for us may actually hurt or harm us in the long run. We can only see the present, but God sees the future. He may deny us things that will harm us or things that won't bring glory to His Name. He may deny us to protect us. What a merciful God.

In 2 Corinthians 11:3 the Bible says, "But I am afraid that just as Eve was deceived by the serpent's cunning, your minds may somehow be led astray from your sincere and pure devotion to Christ." Though I don't want to admit that this verse has rung true in my Christian life, I must confess that I've struggled with that from time to time. Yes, I've been deceived by my own personal wants and desires. Have you? When I get so caught up in my personal desires, I tend to lose focus on the Lord. Why? Because I've started thinking of myself more than God and pride starts settling in. When I struggle with pride it means that I've temporarily put myself on the throne in place of God. Though that can't literally happen, it figuratively occurs in my mind and I must be cautioned. I must realign my thoughts and prioritize God's supremacy as being at the top of my list. I must allow God to renew my mind and change my focus.

Cynthia's book references Psalm 37:4 which says, "Delight yourself in the Lord and he will give you the desires of your heart." Really think about those words as you read that verse again. "Delight yourself in the Lord and he will give you the desires of your heart." If we spend time delighting in the Lord, we'll want whatever He wants for our lives. We'll be willing to submit to His ways rather than our own ways. By default, we will always want what He wants for us when our focus is God. Nothing else will really matter. The things of this world become strangely dim when we turn our eyes upon Jesus.

Charles Spurgeon commented on Psalm 37:4 by saying, "Men who delight in God desire or ask for nothing but what will please God." How many times do we desire or ask for things that are not pleasing to God? *Why* do we desire or ask for things that are not pleasing to God? The answer is simply because we are not delighting in the Person of God. We start delighting in *something* (our personal wants or desires) rather than *Someone* (the Lord Himself). Spurgeon continued on by observing in a little prayer book, "Lord, if what I ask for does not please You, neither would it please me. My desires are put into Your hands to be corrected." Wow, now that's a prayer with the right perspective! A right perspective takes a renewed mind. Have you ever offered the desires of your heart to be corrected by God? What an act of submission and godliness. It's not wrong for us to have personal wants and desires, but we must be willing to hold onto them loosely and be willing to surrender them back to God to do as He chooses with them.

The only way we can do this is by having a transformed mind that stops thinking of ourselves and starts focusing on God. Though it's normal for our human minds to think of ourselves first, we must remember that we became new creatures in Christ the moment we became saved. Since that time, we have been given a new focus—Christ. We have a new Person to live for—Christ. We have new spiritual thoughts and desires—all related to Christ. When we keep the right perspective—Christ—we have new perceptions. We no longer crave to fulfill our own desires. We now desire Christ to be our hearts' desire. It's a 180-degree shift in thinking and there's great freedom that comes with exchanging our ways and thoughts for His.

It takes a transformed mind to focus on what God desires for our lives rather than what we desire for ourselves. It takes the power of the Holy Spirit to redirect our thoughts to be godly. Apart from Him we can do nothing, but with Him, all things are possible. We must always remember that our greatest need is to know that God is enough for us, whether we receive our personal wants and desires or not. We must not let Satan deceive us. God Himself is always enough.

I appreciate the reminder we're given in 2 Corinthians 3:18 that says, "And we, who with unveiled faces all reflect the Lord's glory, are being transformed into his likeness with ever-increasing glory, which comes from the Lord, who is the Spirit." Consider the two words in the middle of that verse that say, "being transformed." Keep in mind that transformation is a process. It's a process that lasts the entire time we're saved while living on this earth. We will never be fully transformed into the image of Christ until we see Him face-to-face. However, we continue to grow into His image while we're here. Our entire Christian lives are a continual transformation process. How gracious of God to be patient with us while He grows us into the image of Christ. What a blessing that

He doesn't rush or delay our transformation process. That is the goodness and grace of God.

Peter emphasized this same idea of maintaining a pure heart and mind to believers. He knew his time on earth was short so he wrote and shared what was on his heart. In 2 Peter 3:1-2, he referenced a letter he'd written which offered hope for believers to grow in Christ. His letters were reminders for believers to stimulate wholesome thinking. Hmmm, what qualifies as *wholesome thinking*?

Peter was instructing believers to, "Recall the words spoken in the past by the holy prophets and the command given by our Lord and Savior through the apostles" (2 Peter 3:2). Peter wanted the believers of his day to keep God's truths on the forefront of their minds. He knew that scoffers and false prophets would come in the last days which might tempt them to forget the truths of God's Word. He didn't want them to be easily swayed.

Peter's words can serve as a reminder to us all in this present day as well. Are you challenged by wholesome thinking? Are you willing to let God transform your mind so you only think on things that are true, noble, right, pure, lovely, admirable, excellent and praiseworthy (Philippians 4:8)? Do you allow Scripture to saturate your mind? If not, ask the Lord to make this a desire of your heart. Cry out to Him with a longing to live in righteousness. Let Him be the guard over your heart and mind. Let Him protect you while He transforms you.

Another way our minds are transformed is through trials. Trials are tests. Our lives are filled with tests all along the way. Sometimes the test set before us is relatively easy to pass, and other times it seems nearly impossible to pass.

I really like what Steven Furtick shared in one of his sermons entitled, "Passing Your Test." Steven is the Lead Pastor of Elevation Church in Charlotte, North Carolina. He shared that many people really don't enjoy taking tests. I certainly fit into that category. Though I did well in school, I clearly remember stressing over upcoming tests. What if I didn't pass? Can any of you relate to that?

Think back to your childhood. All throughout your school years, you were required to take standardized tests in order to prove that you were meeting specific educational standards. For instance, most of us are very familiar with the SAT or ACT tests taken in high school that help decide which post-secondary option may be the best fit for each student. While some embrace those tests as being a great necessity for the next stage of life, others view them as insignificant and a complete waste of time.

Tests can bring about a great deal of anxiety for people. Some individuals freeze up from the pressure, some become anxious over the fear of failure, some either confuse or forget memorized material with the many thoughts swimming in their heads, and some get distracted or lose focus from the ticking clock as precious time drifts away.

While most of us don't personally like taking tests, we like using things that have been tested. For example, the brakes on your car were tested before you purchased it to prove that they work and can keep you safe. Other drivers on the road have been tested before getting their license to prove that they are qualified drivers. Pilots are tested before they can fly commercial planes. Airplane equipment is tested for mechanical issues before a flight takes off. Doctors are tested on the knowledge of the medicines or procedures they'll be offering to their patients, etc. Though we don't necessarily like taking tests, we're most thankful that things—and people—are tested.

Steven quoted that, "Life is a lesson and you will be tested." Isn't that the truth! Life is one big learning center and tests come to show us either what we've learned, or what we're yet to learn. Another quote Steven shared is this, "What is tested can be trusted; what hasn't been tested cannot be trusted." Now just think about that for a minute. As we are tested throughout life, we have the opportunity to experience God at work in our lives. We can see that God is able to get us through the tests we face if we're willing to stay focused on Him. We get to experience His infinite strength and peace that comes as we fully depend upon the Lord to endure and pass each test set before us. Each test reminds us that we have the opportunity to experience God. If we're truly excited about experiencing God, then we won't be fearful or intimidated by any test we face because we've prioritized our perspective. As Psalm 56:3 says, "When I am afraid, I will trust in you." We need to replace our fear of people or circumstances with faith in God.

James 1:2-4 says, "Consider it pure joy, my brothers, whenever you face trials of many kinds, because you know that the testing of your faith develops perseverance. Perseverance must finish its work so that you may be mature and complete, not lacking anything."

While trials aren't necessarily fun, they are necessary. There is a purpose to each and every trial God brings our way. Trials and difficulties are God's way of growing us. He uses trials to transform us to become more and more like Him. Our trials test our faith. When we keep walking by faith through each trial, He produces perseverance in us because He gives us His strength to keep going so we can pass the test. He doesn't want us to fail. He wants us to grow. As we grow, we become mature and complete. We become like Him.

Waiting is a trial. It's a difficulty and a hardship that is unavoidable in this world. As a matter of fact, it seems like we're born into a world that should have a sign saying, "Congratulations, you made it! Now hurry up and wait!"

Regardless of how long or short our wait times are throughout different seasons of life, we can experience joy while we wait because we know that God is working in us and through us. He's teaching us each time we wait. He's transforming our hearts and minds to be fixed on Him. He's teaching us to prioritize Him over the anxiety of our wait. He's using our wait times to remind us that the spiritual and eternal things of life far outweigh the physical and temporal.

What are you waiting for right now in this season of life, dear friends? What is God teaching you as you wait? How are you experiencing God molding and making you into His image while you wait? Are you depending on Him as you wait? If not, ask yourself, "*Well, what are you waiting for?*"

God has every good and perfect attribute that we need in order to be sustained through our waiting periods. He is our Joy, He is our Peace and He is our Patience while we wait. Go to Him and receive all of His goodness. He longs to give Himself to you, but He's waiting for you to come to Him by faith to receive all that He has to offer. When you receive all that He longs to share with you, you will see it become evident in your life. While you depend upon the greatness of God, you will patiently embrace your wait, and the fruit of joy and peace will be abundantly displayed in your life.

As you endure your season of waiting, be willing to let God use that time to transform your heart and mind. Be patient with Him while you wait. He is molding and making you like the potter molds and makes the clay. Keep in mind that God is being patient with you while you are being transformed into His likeness. Receive His patience as you are continually being made into His magnificent image.

Be willing to be tested by the waiting periods of your life and depend upon God to pass the tests for you. He is faithful, and He will do it.

DISCUSSION QUESTIONS:

1. Do you believe that God has your best interest at heart when He denies you what you think you need? Explain.

   _____

   _____

   _____

   _____

2. Psalm 37:4 tells us to, *"Delight yourself in the LORD and he will give you the desires of your heart."* How often do you delight yourself in the Lord rather than delight yourself in personal or worldly desires? Share your thoughts.

   _____

   _____

   _____

   _____

3. Second Corinthians 3:18 says, *"And we, who with unveiled faces all reflect the Lord's glory, are being transformed into his likeness."* How have you seen yourself being transformed by God?

   _____

   _____

   _____

   _____

4. Peter reminded believers of the importance to have *pure hearts and minds*. He emphasized their need to stimulate *wholesome thinking*.

    a. Practically speaking, what can you do to maintain a *pure heart and mind*?

_____

_____

_____

_____

    b. How would you define *wholesome thinking*? Share some examples that would demonstrate *wholesome thinking*.

_____

_____

_____

_____

5. What are you specifically waiting for right now in this season of life?

_____

_____

_____

_____

    a. What is God teaching you as you wait?

_____

_____

_____

_____

b. How are you experiencing God molding and making you into His image while you wait?

_____

_____

_____

_____

c. Are you depending on God as you wait? If so, how? If not, why not?

_____

_____

_____

_____

9

STAY ACTIVE

GOD HAS REMINDED US THROUGHOUT Scripture that our lives are a lifetime of wait. So why are we bothered or surprised by it? Waiting is a natural part of life. No one is exempt from it.

In a previous chapter, we discussed that we are responsible to grow in our relationship with God while we wait. Growth is an action word. It's a verb. It means we need to do something. We must stay active while we wait, rather than become frustrated or discouraged.

Consider this quote, *"Prosperous times produce passive wills."* I heard those words one day as I listened to James MacDonald speak on the radio. His comment really made me stop and think. When life is going well and we're enjoying a time of prosperity here on earth, do we typically find it easier or harder to serve the Lord? If most of us were honest, I think we'd agree that it's harder to serve God when things are going our way. You see, when things are going our way, it's as if we think we've done something right, or have control of life in a certain way, where everything seems to be working out according to our hopes and plans. Since life appears to be running smoothly for us, why would we need God? Isn't it crazy that God tends to be our *last* resort in the good times and our *first* resort in the bad times? But that's not right, and it certainly isn't how God ever intended our relationship to be with Him. It's a challenge, and takes a conscious effort, to acknowledge that we need God in the good times just as much as we need Him in the bad times.

When considering all of the temptations that surround us day after day, have you ever considered how tempting passivity and inactivity can be in our lives? As James MacDonald continued on in his message he said, *"Few of us can handle the temptation of inactivity."* Wow, that's a good point! First of all, I've never really thought of passivity and inactivity as being a temptation. Justifying our passivity and inactivity can become a danger as we consider our personal wants and needs. It's our human nature to fall victim to inactivity while we live in a world that surrounds us with busyness. Many of us might convince ourselves that we deserve periods of inactivity because we need a break from the daily chaos we endure. With the exception of a few highly motivated individuals in this world, our bodies and minds typically choose to do things the quick, easy and most comfortable way. Let's consider a few examples supporting this thought.

Physically, many of us would prefer exercise programs that require minimal sweat, pain or exertion. However, with little work, our minds still want to reap the results of shed pounds and a toned body in the shortest time frame possible. Mentally, we prefer making choices that don't require complicated decisions or require too much time over-analyzing things. Emotionally, we tend to gravitate toward things that make us feel good in the short-term without always thinking of potential long-term consequences or outcomes. Spiritually, our hearts gravitate toward disobedience over obedience because we wrestle with our old sin nature and strong worldly desires.

The act of sin comes natural to us so it's the quickest, easiest and many times the most comfortable choice for us to make. However, we must keep in mind that we are dead to sin but alive to Christ (Romans 6:11). Did you catch that? We are alive to Christ! Though sin is constantly knocking at the door to our hearts, our will is what chooses to open that door and allow sin to enter our lives or not.

Life represents activity. We must learn to wait upon the Lord actively so we don't become a victim of the temptation of *inactivity*. What happens when we become victims of inactivity? The answer is not surprising. When we become inactive we start to doubt, question, grumble and complain. We become negative, critical, quick to judge and are easily swayed by people's opinions rather than God's commands. In his message, James MacDonald went on to say:

> *Few of us can handle the temptation of inactivity. In our passivity, we wander around and start thinking: Do I like my life? Do I like my wife? Do I like my house? Would I be happier in a different house or with a different wife or in another life? So, these are ordinary temptations. What's the remedy? Be proactive in your walk with God. Seek after God with all your heart. None of us can afford to be casual or indifferent about our walk with the Lord.*

When I think of a visual related to staying active while we wait, I think of times when I've been stuck sitting in my car at a stop light. Just because the light turns red and I have to put my brake on doesn't mean I fully shut my car off, right? Who does that?! Though I'm at a standstill, and don't necessarily know how long I'll be there before the light turns green, I wait with anticipation. I'm watchful, expectant, hopeful and eager to go as soon as I receive the new signal.

That's the same way it should be for us as we wait upon the Lord. We should never stop serving or worshiping the Lord just because He's halted an area of our lives. We need to remain watchful. We need to stay hopeful. We need to be ready and willing to go when He says, "Go!" Because at some point, He will expect us to press the gas pedal once again, and we don't want to be sleeping at the wheel when it's time for us to "Go!"

Inactivity needs to be a warning light to us. Danger may lie ahead if we don't acknowledge the apathetic or complacent stage we may be entering. We must stay alert, active, watchful and hopeful as we wait upon the Lord. We must keep exercising our minds and hearts by keeping our eyes fixed on Christ and by reading, meditating and sharing God's Word with others. Stay alert as you wait, dear friends, and keep a conscious mind.

Noah Built the Ark

Think back to the story of Noah. This man was told by God to make an ark of cypress wood that was 450 feet long, 75 feet wide and 45 feet high. My Bible commentary relates the size of the ark as being one and a half football fields long and as high as a four-story building. Now that's more like the size of a cruise ship than a boat!

Do you think that being commanded to build a ginormous boat in the middle of the desert may have seemed like an outlandish request of him from God? Not to mention the fact that Noah was rapidly approaching 600 years old when he first got assigned this task. God would allow 120 years for the boat to be built before He dealt with the wickedness of the world. Wasn't Noah too old to construct this type of monstrosity in the middle of dry land in the first place? Shouldn't he have been at the stage of contemplating retirement rather than construction? The answer is, "No." God had a plan and purpose for Noah and his family just as He has for us. This assignment would actually be an opportunity for them to worship God. When we consider this situation, a question should come to our minds. "If God brings an outlandish assignment our way, do we believe in Him enough to act on His plans without delay?"

The idea of building an ark may have seemed a bit crazy, and we can't help but wonder, "What did Noah do for 120 years while he waited for God to bring the rain that was promised? Did he question the seriousness of God's request and allow time for God to change His mind? Did he sit around day after day waiting for the storm clouds to roll in so he could be certain that the rain would come? After all, that would justify that the building of the ark was worth his time and effort, right?" Of course not. Noah got to work immediately after being commanded by the Lord to get the job done. He diligently built the ark God instructed of him so he and his family could be spared when the floodgates of heaven opened on the dry land.

Scripture tells us that, "Noah found favor in the eyes of the Lord" (Genesis 6:8). We are also told that, "Noah was a righteous man, blameless among the people of his time, and he walked with God" (Genesis 6:9). Isn't that a tremendous description to be given as a follower of God? Noah was active. He walked with God. There's nothing idle about walking with the Lord. When we read the story of Noah and the ark, it almost seems ridiculous that God would take so long to bring the rains which would wipe out the wickedness on the earth. But as 1 Peter 3:20 reminds us, "God waited patiently in the days of Noah while the ark was being built."

Noah lived to be 950 years old. He was one of the oldest men listed in the Bible to have ever lived. God allowed 120 years for Noah to prepare himself and his family from disaster. That meant that nearly 13 percent of Noah's life was spent building a huge boat in the middle of a desert where it didn't rain. When you consider that percentage, doesn't it seem like God wasted a significant portion of Noah's life? Why would God allow such a long time of hard work and labor for a righteous man who had found favor in the eyes of the Lord?

We need to remember that God allows all the time necessary for His plans and purposes to be carried out according to His will. Sure, God could've spoken the ark into existence for Noah and his family if He wanted to, but that wouldn't have allowed an opportunity for Noah to demonstrate his faith in God among a community of wicked and evil people. These people needed to know God. No one would've seen the promise of God fulfilled in the same way if God hadn't been so patient. If God wouldn't have waited the full 120 years before allowing the rains to come down, the flooding rains would've come too early and Noah's family would've been wiped out along with everyone and everything around him. How gracious of God to be patient with His creation.

God allowed time for the wicked to repent and trust in Him. That's 120 years He set aside for the wicked to repent and turn to Him. Again, I must reiterate, what a patient God! He allowed Noah time to prepare his family for safety. It's amazing to think that Noah was testifying of his faith in God every day as he endured 120 years of hard labor and toil. Imagine how crazy the wicked must have thought Noah was for piecing together a humungous boat in the middle of the desert where it never rained, simply because God told him to do so. Who does that? Noah did, that's who. He served God faithfully as He waited for the promised results from God to literally rain down from heaven. He knew God's plans and purposes would prevail, he just didn't know when. Noah simply knew his job was to stay active and obey God's commands. How about us? Do we care more about how long we'll have to obey God in a difficult circumstance, or do we care most about obeying God despite the length of time and circumstance?

Activity is important for our body, mind, soul and spirit. We know that physical exercise is an important element for the health of our bodies. But what type of activity is good for our soul and spirit? This answer may surprise you, but let's look to see what God's Word commands us in 1 Peter 1:13, "Prepare your minds *for action*." How do we prepare our minds? Again, looking to Scripture, we find a very familiar verse in Psalm 46:10 that commands us how we should prepare our minds. It says, "Be still and *know* that I am God." We must know in our minds that He is God. It takes a clear, conscious mind to do that intently and purposefully. When our minds are focused on the right thing, our actions follow by default. Our minds steer our actions.

But doesn't that seem like an oxy-moron? *Prepare* while *being still*. Though this may seem nearly impossible, try this exercise. Get yourself into a quiet place where you can be free from worldly distractions and start mediating on just one of the many attributes and promises of God. The list of God's attributes and promises are lengthy so I have included just a short list of them below to help get our minds going in the right direction.

Pick just one of the words from the following list and think about how important it is for us to know that word which describes God.

Attributes of God:

Love	Faithful	Refuge	Friend
Mercy	Truth	Strength	Just
Grace	Kind	Hope	Compassion
Peace	Life	Redeemer	Omnipotent
Righteous	Savior	Creator	Omniscient
Holy	Almighty	Forgiving	Everlasting
Sovereign	Sufficient	Deliverer	Able

Consider the word you selected and ask yourself a few questions. What does that attribute mean to you personally? How is that attribute of God important in your life right now? How does meditating on that attribute make you want to respond to God right now?

Along with the attributes of God, the Bible is full of numerous promises from God. Choose one of the following promises to meditate on, or consider another promise that you've already stored in your heart, and reflect on that for several minutes.

Promises of God:

- I have loved you with an everlasting love (Jeremiah 31:3)

- I have made you and I will carry you (Isaiah 46:4)

- My mercies are new every morning (Lamentations 3:22-23)

- I am the resurrection and the life (John 11:25)

- I am close to the brokenhearted (Psalm 34:18)

- I am with you wherever you go (Joshua 1:9)

- I will strengthen you and help you (Isaiah 41:10)

- I am slow to anger and abounding in love (Psalm 103:8)

- I will instruct you and teach you in the way that you should go (Psalm 32:8)

- I will fight for you (Exodus 14:14)

- I will revive the spirit of the lowly and revive the heart of the contrite (Isaiah 57:15)

- I am the way, the truth and the life (John 14:6)

- I will advise you and watch over you (Psalm 32:8)

- I am the Lord and I do not change (Malachi 3:6)

- I will take revenge; I will pay them back (Romans 12:19)

- I will rescue those who love me (Psalm 91:14-16)

What thoughts came to your mind as you meditated on those words? Which of God's many promises speaks to you loudest right now? How does that promise make you want to respond to God? How can you apply that promise to your life right now?

A favorite verse of mine that I often meditate on is Zephaniah 3:17:

> *The LORD your God is with you, he is mighty to save. He will take great delight in you, he will quiet you with his love, he will rejoice over you with singing.*

Reread that verse a few more times and really concentrate on each phrase. Aren't those words so encouraging when you take time to let them sink in? He is with you. Do you really believe that? Apart from Him there is no god. Only He is mighty to save. God promises in that verse to delight in us, quiet us and rejoice over us with singing. How comforting and humbling. We don't deserve that from our heavenly Father, but those actions demonstrate His love for us. What a gracious and compassionate God we serve. There is no one like Him. We need to be thankful ... so very thankful. And when our hearts are overflowing with thankfulness, we worship the Lord by actively serving Him, and others around us, with gladness. God's Word, His attributes and His promises, are all vital aspects for us to consider in order for us to stay active while we wait.

THE BATTLEFIELD OF OUR MINDS

One of the greatest things we battle in life is our minds. It's difficult for us to filter all of the information and thoughts that bombard our minds on a daily basis. We see and hear things we wish we could avoid. Even with the greatest intentions, we can struggle by letting negative thoughts clutter our minds while letting God's truth slip away from us. That's why God knew we'd need the reminder of 1 Peter 1:13, "Prepare your minds for action." He knows that our minds are a constant battlefield for us. He knows how weak our flesh is. He knows that we, just like the apostle Paul, struggle with the tug-of-war that comes from spiritually wanting to do the right thing but humanly choosing to do the wrong thing from time to time.

Because of that, God reminded us of our need to prepare our minds for action. This means choosing godliness over worldliness, holiness over humanness, obedience over disobedience. We need to act on truth, and truth is both the Person of God, as well as the written Word of God. We need to prepare our minds to act on whom we know God is (His attributes), and we need to prepare to act on what the truth of His Word promises.

The struggle comes when we hear a voice questioning our choice of obedience. That's the voice of doubt, also known as Satan. The pull of his voice will quickly and craftily enter our minds if we aren't prepared to identify it and turn from it immediately. As humans, we are quick to forget the truth of God's Word. The temptation to doubt is powerful, but we must remember that God has all the power we need to ward off any doubt. He is our power, our strength and our shield. We need to make it a priority to actively keep God's truths at the forefront of our minds, lest we quickly forget.

Lamentations 3:25-26 says, "The LORD is good to those whose hope is in him; to the one who seeks him; it is good to wait quietly for the salvation of the LORD." Note that we are told to wait quietly. To many of us, we can misinterpret the word quietly to mean inactivity. We need to be careful to understand that the word *quiet* is referring to the state of our heart, not the state of our being.

Quiet is referring to the peace, comfort and rest that comes from God alone as we cast our cares upon Him. We don't have to struggle with the burdens and bondage that anxiety and stress can bring. We can enjoy complete freedom in Christ as our hearts take comfort in who He is rather than in what is going on around us. "It is for freedom that Christ has set us free. Stand firm, then, and do not let yourselves be burdened again by a yoke of slavery" (Galatians 5:1). May your heart be calm and your joy be full as you actively serve Him while you quietly wait upon the Lord.

FAITH EXPRESSING ITSELF THROUGH LOVE

As I was reading Scripture and writing this morning, God revealed a very impactful verse to me that I don't recall ever meditating on before. It's Galatians 5:6b and it says, "… The only thing that counts is faith expressing itself through love." I love the word *express*. What a dynamic action word. It challenges me not to be passive with my faith. We are not to be quiet with our faith. We are to be bold and confident. My faith in God is to be expressed, but it needs to be expressed through love or it doesn't count. We have permission, and an expectation, by God to express our faith through love. That love we've received is from God through Jesus Christ, His Son. We express our faith in God by loving others.

God rewards me for demonstrating my love for Him. I like to think that any, and all, of the rewards I will reap in heaven one day will be considered "love rewards." These love rewards are intended to be laid before the feet of Jesus when we reside in heaven one glorious day.

God blesses and rewards faith that has been demonstrated through loving others. Each demonstration of godly love represents self-sacrifice. Self-sacrifice represents Christ. As Romans 5:8 says, "… God demonstrates His own love for us in this: While we were still sinners, Christ died for us." Why did Christ die for us? He died so that we could be filled with His unfailing love and, in return, pour that love into the lives of others. We need to continuously die to self in order to demonstrate our faith in God and allow His love to be shared with the world. Don't hold back. Don't be shy. Express your faith by loving on others while you wait and be encouraged by the rewards that God longs to give you.

Sometimes I can get so caught up in *what* I'm doing, or what I'm supposed to be doing, that I overlook the *who* that I'm representing. Who I represent as a Christian is Jesus Christ. We must make a conscious effort to recognize the love of Christ in all that we do. It will never really matter what any of us are doing if we don't do it with the love of Christ. May we never grow weary of learning to love like Jesus.

While we wait upon the Lord, we must practice loving the people

God has brought into our lives. Our waiting periods give us time to live out the commands He has taught us through Scripture. When we live out His Word, we stay active. Just like with physical activity, spiritual activity allows us to keep our minds and hearts in a healthy state and will prepare us to meet Jesus face-to-face one glorious day.

I love this quote from Vivian Greene that someone shared with me several years ago. It says, "Life's not about waiting for the storm to pass ... it's about learning to dance in the rain." Isn't that great? Satan wants us to get discouraged during our times of wait. He wants us to lose our hope in the Lord. He wants us to sit idle so we don't serve the Lord, or others, while we wait. However, this quote reminds me that if we sit around and become idle while we wait, we're wasting the time God has gifted to us to testify of Him. We'll simply miss out on all the goodness and blessings that God intended for us while we wait. We have a choice to make. We can either sit by the window sill waiting for the storm clouds to pass us by, or we can put our rain boots on and joyfully jump in the puddles. My friends, let's choose to dance in the rain!

DISCUSSION QUESTIONS:

1. Have you ever viewed passivity and inactivity as being temptations in your life? Explain.

   _____

   _____

   _____

   _____

2. When life is going well, and you're enjoying a time of prosperity, do you typically find it easier or harder to serve the Lord during that time? Why?

   _____

   _____

   _____

   _____

3. Romans 6:11 reminds us that we are, *"Dead to sin but alive to God in Christ Jesus."*

   a. What do those words mean to you?

   _____

   _____

   _____

   _____

   b. Does your life exemplify that you are indeed, *"Alive to Christ?"* How?

   _____

   _____

   _____

   _____

4. Consider God's command to Noah to build the ark. Noah knew it was his job to stay active and obey God's command even though he didn't know how long it would take to complete the ark. Do you care more about how long you'll have to obey God during a difficult task or circumstance, or do you care most about obeying God, despite the time and tasks you may have to endure? Share your thoughts.

    _____

    _____

    _____

    _____

5. Select one of the *"Attributes of God"* listed in this chapter on a previous page and write it down:_____

    a. What does that attribute really mean to you?

    _____

    _____

    _____

    _____

    b. How is that important in your life right now?

    _____

    _____

    _____

    _____

    c. How does that make you want to respond to God?

    _____

    _____

    _____

    _____

6. Select one of the verses related to the *"Promises of God"* listed in this chapter.

    a. Write the words to the verse in the space below and share what thoughts come to your mind as you meditate on those words.

_____

_____

_____

_____

    b. How does that promise make you want to respond to God? Why?

_____

_____

_____

_____

    c. How can you apply that promise to your life right now?

_____

_____

_____

_____

7. When God commands you to do something, do you typically believe His plan enough to start acting on it right away, or are you cautious, waiting for more clarity? Explain.

_____

_____

_____

_____

10

PREPARE

SCRIPTURE IS FILLED WITH EXAMPLES demonstrating how people of the Bible prepared as they waited for a variety of situations to come to fruition. It's easy to prepare when we anticipate an exciting outcome. But when we foresee discouragement or destruction on the horizon, we tend to get gripped by fear and overlook our need to prepare. Regardless of what your future holds, don't waste your wait. Prepare to keep your eyes fixed on God and be willing to be obedient to His call.

PAUL PREPARED TO DIE

In Acts 20:22 we read that Paul was compelled by the Holy Spirit to go to Jerusalem even though he did not know what was going to happen to him there. Though he was uncertain as to what he could expect when he reached the city, it's interesting to note that there was one thing Paul was indeed aware of as he traveled. As he stated, "I only know that in every city the Holy Spirit warns me that prison and hardships are facing me" (vs 23).

Wow! The only thing Paul was aware of was that the promise of prison and hardships awaited him. That, in itself, is enough for anyone in their right mind to say, "Cancel my trip!" Who purposely goes where trouble lurks?! Not many are up for that task. In our simple minds, we probably would have encouraged Paul *not* to go to Jerusalem knowing that hardships were the only guarantee he'd been given. You see, as human beings, we typically crave an easy life … one without trials, tribulations and strife. Most of us aren't eager to sign up for opportunities that require a lot of blood, sweat and tears. Those go against our fleshly desires. But that wasn't the case for Paul. Paul was a man of God who knew without a doubt that hardships were part of a servant's life unto the Lord.

Considering the idea of being a servant, read what Paul wrote with great confidence and boldness in 2 Corinthians 6:4-10:

> Rather, as servants of God we commend ourselves in every way: in great endurance; in troubles, hardships and distresses; in beatings, imprisonments and riots; in hard work, sleepless nights and hunger; in purity, understanding, patience and kindness; in the Holy Spirit and in sincere love; in truthful speech and in the power of God; with weapons of righteousness in the right hand and in the left; through glory and dishonor, bad report and good report; genuine, yet regarded as impostors; known, yet regarded as unknown; dying, and yet we live on; beaten, and yet not killed; sorrowful, yet always rejoicing; poor, yet making many rich; having nothing, and yet possessing everything.

What an incredible statement of ownership and responsibility Paul accepted for his Christian life. He was a servant of God. Paul was able to endure whatever lay ahead of him in Jerusalem, just like he did in all of the other cities and countries he traveled to, simply because he had mentally prepared himself to focus on one important truth … in Christ alone he had everything. Paul was willing to surrender *all* of himself simply because he knew that he had already received everything he'd ever need by trusting in the Lord Jesus for his eternal life. Now *that's* living out the freedom we have in Christ! Paul considered his life worth nothing to him. His only desire was to finish the race and complete the task the Lord Jesus had given him. And that specific task was to testify to the gospel of God's grace (Acts 20:24).

It was with this servant attitude, despite the tears that accompanied him, that Paul headed to Jerusalem knowing he would never see the faces of his dear friends, or the elders of Ephesus, again.

Paul met other disciples and Christian brothers along his way. They, too, urged him not to go on to Jerusalem. But because Paul was mentally prepared for the journey, he knelt with them in prayer and carried on.

Paul met a prophet named Agabus who had come down from Judea while Paul was staying with Philip, the evangelist, in Caesarea. Acts 21:11 says that Agabus took Paul's belt, tied his own hands and feet with it and said, "The Holy Spirit says, 'In this way the Jews of Jerusalem will bind the owner of this belt and will hand him over to the Gentiles.'" This news, of course, caused the people nearby to plead that Paul would not continue his journey up to Jerusalem. Imagine loved ones pleading for you not to go somewhere. Imagine knowing the danger that lies ahead. Imagine the fear and anxiety that could be seeping into your mind encouraging you to put an abrupt halt to your trip.

But then imagine being mentally prepared for this divine appointment set before you from God. Paul was prepared. He demonstrated this so beautifully through one of his most profound statements recorded in Scripture when he answered the people by saying, "Why are you weeping and breaking my heart? I am ready not only to be bound, but also to die in Jerusalem for the name of the Lord Jesus" (Acts 21:13).

Paul was ready. He had mentally prepared for this trip of no return. He knew what lay before him and he accepted it with great confidence from God. Paul rejoiced in the fact that, "To live is Christ, and to die is gain" (Philippians 1:21). What a testimony of faith as he waited upon the Lord. He waited with great hope, anticipation and perseverance so that nothing would stand in his way while he carried on as a servant of the Lord.

ESTHER'S REQUEST TO THE KING

Esther was a beautiful young virgin woman who was made queen by King Xerxes. The king reigned over 127 provinces stretching from

India to Cush, including the citadel of Susa. Esther was put into this royal position after Queen Vashti had disrespected the king and was stripped of her noble crown. What the king didn't know about Esther was that she was a Jew. She had been adopted by her cousin, Mordecai, who was a Jew from the tribe of Benjamin. Mordecai brought Esther in and raised her when her father and mother died years earlier. Mordecai had been carried into exile from Jerusalem by Nebuchadnezzar king of Babylon and inherited an official position among the Jewish captives that kept him around the palace. Esther had kept her family background and nationality a secret from the others in the community, just as Mordecai had told her to do.

As time went on, King Xerxes honored a man named Haman and gave him a seat of honor higher than that of all the other nobles. All the royal officials at the king's gate knelt down and paid honor to Haman as the king had commanded them. All of the nobles, that is, except Mordecai. When Haman realized Mordecai wouldn't kneel down or pay honor to him, he was enraged. Knowing that Mordecai was a Jew, Haman not only wanted Mordecai to die, but he wanted all of the Jewish people living throughout the kingdom of Xerxes to die as well.

Haman addressed the king and told him that there were certain people scattered among the provinces of the kingdom whose customs were different from all the other people. He was clear to let the king know that these different customs didn't line up with obeying the king's laws. Haman recommended that it was not in the king's best interest to tolerate these altered customs and suggested that those who practiced them be destroyed. The king allowed Haman to do as he pleased with the people. However, King Xerxes didn't realize that this would mean killing Queen Esther, with whom he found great favor.

A script was written and sent out with an order to all the king's provinces to destroy, kill and annihilate all the Jews, regardless of their age, gender or status. The order was written in the name of King Xerxes and sealed with his own ring. The city of Susa was bewildered when they heard the news. There was great mourning among the Jews along with fasting, weeping and wailing.

Esther soon found out about the plot to kill all of the Jews and Mordecai urged her to go into the king's presence to beg for mercy and plead with him for her people. Though she was alarmed by the situation, and tensions were high, she knew that there was a proper way and time to approach the king. The immediacy of addressing this issue was urgent, but she was wise in knowing that it was in everyone's best interest for her to wait. So Esther waited purposefully. She knew she must prepare to meet the king for such a time as this.

Put yourself in Esther's shoes for a moment and imagine the stressful situation this was for both her, as well as the entire Jewish community. She was their only hope in order for their lives to be spared. But Esther was only allowed to approach the king in one of two ways. She either had to be summoned by the king himself, or the king would have to extend the gold scepter to her. If she approached him under any other circumstances, she would be put to death.

So how did Queen Esther prepare under such difficult circumstances? Though she was hopeful for an outcome where all of the Jews would be spared, the king had no idea that she was a Jew herself. How would he receive that information? As she prepared her heart for that defining moment, she sent a reply to Mordecai telling him to gather all of the Jews in Susa and fast for her. They were not to eat or drink for three full days. While the Jews were fasting for Esther, she fasted for them as well. After that time, she agreed to go to the king. Knowing that approaching the king in this way would be against the law, she prepared her mind to willingly commit to these words, "And if I perish, I perish" (Esther 4:16b).

Imagine that. Esther was prepared to die in order to help save the lives of her people. However, she wasn't willing to die without preparing first. What did she do while she waited for the right time to approach the king? She fasted for three days and she planned her steps out carefully in order to have a chance at redemption for her Jewish community. Imagine the many thoughts that must have been circling through her mind as she contemplated all of the possibilities of how this situation could unfold. Would the king extend the gold scepter to her? Would the king be angered that Esther never initially told him she was a Jew? Would the king spare the lives of both her and the Jews? The thoughts, questions and potential outcomes that flooded her mind must have been overwhelming.

On the third day of the fast, Esther stood in front of the king's hall. As King Xerxes sat on his royal throne facing the entrance, he was pleased with her and held out the gold scepter that was in his hand. What a relief that he was willing to receive her. Esther approached the royal throne and touched the tip of the scepter.

While the king was anxious to hear Esther's request, she held back and took things a different direction. Instead of presenting the request for her Jewish people to be spared, she invited the king and Haman to attend a banquet that she had prepared. Isn't that interesting? While Esther waited those three days to approach the king, she determined that even more wait time would be necessary. So, she creatively prepared a banquet for the two men rather than rush into the main reason she had wanted to approach the king in the first place. This reminds me of a saying I've come across multiple times lately that states, "Do the important over the urgent."

What comes to mind when you read that saying? How quick are we to rush into doing the urgent things of life at the expense of doing the important things of life? Sure, there are times when we must act quickly because an urgent matter needs to be addressed. But are there times when we're overlooking important things simply because something more urgent is staring us right in the face?

For example, maybe you're on a phone call encouraging another individual through a difficult situation when your toddler walks up and says, "I'm hungry!" Do you shorten your phone call just to make a snack for your child because their request sounds urgent? They will be fine if they're told they have to wait. On the other hand, if you're on that same phone call and your child gets hurt while playing outside, it would make sense for you to end your call quickly in order to take care of your child's need as soon as possible. And that's where the real question comes into play. What, or where, is the greatest need?

As stated in a book entitled *Uncommon Sense* by Nido R. Qubein, President of High Point University, this idea of focusing on the important over the urgent was addressed. Qubein commented, "Urgent choices are choices that demand immediate attention. Important choices are those that move us toward our goals. The fewer urgent choices we have, the more time and energy we have to focus on the important ones."

We must really think through and analyze the things that are most important in life before we waste too much time addressing the things that are simply screaming for our attention. And that's exactly what Esther did while she waited. She prepared to prioritize the most important matter and approach concerning her people. Yes, it was urgent that she approach the king, but she was wise to know that the most important decision she'd make was in terms of *how* she would approach the king.

While sparing the lives of the Jews was of greatest urgency, Esther knew that it was of vital importance for her to maintain favor with the king. After all, he was the one who would make that defining, critical decision as to whether they would all live or die. Esther was willing to wait for the most important pieces to fall into place before rushing into what appeared to be the most urgent matter at hand. What a wise woman. There is much to be learned from Esther's example as she prepared her words and her actions while she waited.

At the banquet, the king asked Esther, "What is your request?" (Esther 5:3). Not only was he interested to hear her thoughts, he also confirmed it would be given to her. Rather than give him a specific answer, Esther invited the king and Haman to another banquet that she planned to prepare for them the following day. Esther agreed to answer the king's question at that time. So, the king and Haman arranged to dine with Queen Esther once again.

At the second banquet, the king asked the queen, "What is your petition? What is your request?" (Esther 5:6). King Xerxes continued on letting her know that whatever it was, it would be given to her. After all of Esther's preparations and purposeful wait, it was now time. Esther was ready to answer the king. She responded, "If I have found favor with you, O king, and if it pleases your majesty, grant me my life—this is my petition. And spare my people—this is my request. For I and my people have been sold for destruction and slaughter and annihilation. If we had merely been sold as male and female slaves, I would have kept quiet, because no such distress would justify disturbing the king" (Esther 7:3-4).

As the rest of the story unfolds, we find out that Haman is called out and killed for plotting to destroy the Jews. Mordecai was presented with the king's signet ring and was appointed over Haman's estate. The evil plan devised against the Jews was overturned and the lives of the Jews were spared. The king's revised edict granted the Jews in every city the right to assemble and protect themselves. There was great happiness, joy, gladness and honor in the city of Susa as the Jews celebrated victory with feasting and celebrating.

I appreciated what my Bible commentary shared regarding a brief summary of a portion of this story. It said, "God was in control, yet Mordecai and Esther had to act. We cannot understand how both can be true at the same time, and yet they are. God chooses to work through those willing to act for Him. We should pray as if all depended on God and act as if all depended on us. We should avoid two extremes: doing nothing, and feeling that we must do everything."

Like Esther, we must be patient and wait upon the Lord. We must let Him determine our steps and act upon those steps with great fervor and dedication once they are revealed to us. Though this may sound extreme, we must be willing to be obedient unto the Lord and have the same response as Esther when she said, "And if I perish, I perish" (Esther 4:16b). Paul reflected that same response as he made his way to Jerusalem. But no matter how discouraging a foreseeable outcome may appear, may we always remember that God is our Victor over death! Only life awaits those who are found in Christ.

Habakkuk Prepared for Difficult Times

We can learn much about waiting from the prophet Habakkuk in the Old Testament. In Habakkuk 3:16-19, we learn that Habakkuk was waiting for difficult times to come. Though most of us don't welcome difficulties, they're realities we must all face from time to time. Habakkuk, a prophet of God, was no exception. What's most interesting is how he prepared to endure the upcoming trials headed his way.

Habakkuk lived and prophesied in Judah. Babylon was becoming the dominant world power. The Babylonians were as wicked as the Assyrians, loved to collect prisoners, were proud of their warfare tactics and trusted in their military strength. Habakkuk was saddened by the violence and corruption he saw around him and so he poured his heart out to God. He had questions and concerns related to, "Why does God often seem indifferent in the face of evil? Why do evil people seem to go unpunished?" He was appalled that God would use a nation more wicked than Judah to punish his own country. But despite his questions and lack of understanding God's ways, He kept trusting and communing with God.

Here's a glimpse of Habakkuk's heartfelt prayer as he waited upon the Lord while the destruction of the Babylonians was knocking at Judah's door:

Habakkuk 3:16-19

I heard and my heart pounded, my lips quivered at the sound; decay crept into my bones, and my legs trembled. Yet I will wait patiently for the day of calamity to come on the nation invading us. Though the fig tree does not bud and there are no grapes on the vines, though the olive crop fails and the fields produce no food, though there are no sheep in the pen and no cattle in the stalls, yet I will rejoice in the LORD, I will be joyful in God my Savior. The Sovereign LORD is my strength; he makes my feet like the feet of a deer, he enables me to go on the heights.

The Babylonians were coming. Disaster and despair were in sight. Despite the fact that hard times were coming his way, Habakkuk made a choice to wait patiently on the Lord rather than get alarmed over something he had no control over. Though he was experiencing human emotions and fears, he chose not to let them consume him. He learned to verbalize and express his insecurities to the Lord. He prayed his heart to God.

Habakkuk was determined to let God reign over his life and he was able to rest in the assurance of his Almighty God. Habakkuk was able to remain confident in the fact that, though there would soon be no fruit on the vines, no food produced in the fields and no cattle in the stalls, he would rejoice in the Lord and be joyful in the God of his salvation because he knew that the Lord God would be his strength. Isn't that amazing? Habakkuk chose the higher road. It's the road less traveled. He chose the road that had a God-centered focus rather than a self-centered one. He chose to commune with God.

It's obvious that Habakkuk was dealing with human fears. He admitted the realities that his heart pounded, his lips quivered and his legs trembled, as military forces neared. He could have easily become gripped by spiritual fear as he prepared for the difficult days that lay ahead, but he determined in his heart to let God be his strength. What a tremendous example this man is to us in this present day, as to how we need to wait upon the Lord. Difficult and unpleasant circumstances will always be present during different periods of our lives. But the key to our wait, dear friends, is that we rejoice in the Lord ... not our circumstances. We must prepare ourselves to have this mindset while we wait.

Pour your heart out to Him as you wait. Pray your deepest thoughts to God. Tell Him your fears and insecurities. Be real and vulnerable before God. Release your anxieties to Him so He can comfort your heart. Do everything that's necessary to prepare your heart for obedience as you wait.

WHAT TO EXPECT WHEN YOU'RE EXPECTING

Previously, we discussed the idea that while we wait, we are called to anticipate, prepare, and expect that God is working in our lives. This reminds me of two all-familiar books that many parents read when they find out they're pregnant—especially with their first child. One of the books is called *What to Expect When You're Expecting?* and the other is called *What to Expect the First Year.* Are you as familiar with these as I am?

I received copies of both of these books when I was pregnant with my first child. I read them from cover to cover. I was eager to know what to expect during my pregnancy every step of the way and I wanted to be the best, healthiest mom possible when my little one arrived. I wanted to know how my body was going to change over the next nine months, as well as how my baby would be developing at the same time. (One of my first questions to the nurse was, "Are you sure everyone's stomach can stretch that far?!?!") It was exciting to find out how my baby and I were going to grow together.

The reason so many first-time moms and dads read these books is because they want to be well-equipped and prepared for this tiny gift from God that will soon be snuggled up to them in only a few short months. For many parents, this gift will be with them for a lifetime. It's understandable why a mother or father would want to read up on the best way they can care for their child throughout the various stages of development that lie ahead.

If we apply this concept to our spiritual lives, we need to prepare our hearts in the same way. God has gifted us with a book as well to best equip us for the spiritual journey we're on as we anticipate the return for His children. That incredible, best-selling book is called the Bible. It has everything we need to walk through this life in righteousness until we meet Jesus face-to-face. The Bible is our guide, our instructional manual and our encouragement to obey God and stay in a healthy relationship with Him every step of the way.

As God's Word says in John 17:17, "... your word is truth." Yes, every word in the Bible is true and we need to saturate our minds and hearts with as much of God's truth as possible. God's Word is to consume us and fill us so we can stand in victory against the schemes of the devil and the evil forces of this world. God is clear to us in John 16:33 that, "In this world you *will* have trouble" (emphasis added). However, God has overcome the world. Though our troubles may disappoint us, they will not destroy us. The Bible encourages us how we can experience the peace of God through our troubling circumstances. We do not have to fear or be discouraged, for God is our Victor through every trial. Reading and meditating on God's Word helps prepare our hearts and minds on how we can handle difficult circumstances when they come. Because rest assured ... they *will* come.

The Bible is the only reliable resource to help us live our lives in a way that is honoring and pleasing to the Lord. It's also the only resource that gives us first-hand accounts as to the character, promises and works of God. What's even more amazing is that the Bible tells us what to expect as we anticipate the miraculous return of Christ in the days ahead. The Bible is our spiritual book of *What to Expect When You're Expecting.*

Dear friends, are you expecting the return of Christ? Are you anticipating His arrival as eagerly as you may have anticipated the birth of your first child? Are you preparing your heart and mind to see Jesus face-to-face? God has gifted us with His Word to encourage us each and every day as we live here on earth. Read it with great anticipation, eagerness and fervor. With fear and trembling, Habakkuk prepared for the disaster that lay ahead of him. Out of respect and reverence for the Lord, Habakkuk also prepared his heart for obedience despite the disaster. May we follow his example and prepare our hearts in the same way as we wait upon the Lord.

Discussion Questions:

1. When you become aware that conflict, hardship or difficulties await you, are you quick to get discouraged or are you able to remain confident in the Lord? Explain.

2. What do the words from Philippians 1:21 really mean to you when Paul said, *"For to me, to live is Christ and to die is gain?"*

3. Consider the words *urgent* and *important*.

   a. How often do you prioritize what's *urgent* over what's *important*? Share your thoughts.

   b. Share some specific examples of things you would classify as being *urgent* and *important*? How do they differ?

4. Like Queen Esther, have you ever been willing to wait even longer than you expected until you truly had clear direction from the Lord? If so, what was that experience like?

_____

_____

_____

_____

5. How are you doing in your current stage of life reading, studying and meditating on God's Word? Do you have a fervent heart to grow in the Lord so you are prepared to keep your eyes fixed on Him no matter what situations lie ahead? Be open and honest as you share your heart.

_____

_____

_____

_____

6. Is there someone you currently have in your life who holds you accountable in your walk with God so you are encouraged to keep growing in Him? If so, write out a brief prayer thanking God for them. If not, write out a brief prayer asking God to bring someone like that into your life.

_____

_____

_____

_____

11

OBEY GOD

GOD EXPECTS US TO OBEY Him whether we are waiting upon Him, or whether we are acting upon His direction for our lives. Not only does God expect us to obey Him, He expects us to obey Him fully. There is no partial obedience with God. There are two commands mentioned in Deuteronomy 11:13 that all followers of God are expected to live out to the full. Let's review these verses together:

> So if you faithfully obey the commands I am giving you today—to love the LORD your God and to serve him with all your heart and with all your soul ...

The first command is for us to love the Lord our God. That doesn't mean love Him a little or love Him a lot. It means that in order to faithfully obey Him, we must love Him to the full. We are to love God with every ounce of our being.

The second command is to serve Him with all our heart and with all our soul. Notice that this verse references the word *all* rather than *some*. We are faithfully obeying the Lord when we serve Him with all of our heart and with all of our soul. Yet in our humanness, we're prone to become comfortable by giving God *some* of ourselves ... some of our time ... some of our tithe ... some of our energy ... some of our service. We justify the fact that He's lucky to be getting at least some of us, rather than none of us at all. Besides, giving Him our all may become uncomfortable. He wouldn't want that for His children, right? Wrong. We are to give God our all, no matter what the task, no matter what the cost.

THE GOLDEN CALF

Let's look at a familiar biblical story where God's people got impatient and chose not to wait any longer. It's found in Exodus 32 and it's the story about the golden calf. Let me set the stage for you.

Back in Exodus 24, Moses, Aaron and several other leaders were instructed to go to the foot of Mount Sinai and worship the Lord. All of them, except for Moses, were to worship God at a distance. Only Moses himself was given permission to approach the Lord by actually going up the mountain. This was when the Lord was going to give Moses the tablets of stone, which were the Ten Commandments. Moses went up the mountain and stayed on it for forty days and forty nights.

Now keep in mind that before Moses went up the mountain, he prepared the Israelites of what the Lord's words and laws were regarding this event. They responded by saying, "Everything the LORD has said we will do." As Moses continued on, reminding them of the things the Lord told them to do, they responded again by saying, "We will do everything the LORD has said; we will obey" (Exodus 24:3,7). Multiple times the Israelites verbally committed that they would follow and obey the Lord's commands.

As Moses, and Joshua his aide, set out to go up the mountain of God, Moses said to the elders, "Wait here for us until we come back to you" (vs 14). You see, Moses didn't tell Aaron and the other elders how long he'd be gone because he simply didn't know that for himself. It's not that Moses withheld that information from the others. The fact was that the Lord hadn't revealed those details to him. All he knew was that God had called him to come, while God told the others to wait. Both were to act on what the Lord commanded them to do.

Have you ever been in that type of a situation before? Have you ever been in a relationship with someone where they were given a task or assignment and you just had to wait for them to complete it? I have. It's pretty easy on the front end to tell someone that we're fine waiting for them to finish something, or return from somewhere, but as the days linger on, and there may become a lack of communication from the other individual, the wait can become both frustrating and burdensome. We may get to the point where we just want to move on with our own lives and give up on waiting for the other person.

To make this example more personal, consider individuals close to you that might be serving in the military. Imagine that they get sent out on assignment to go overseas to a country where there has been much conflict. They tell you that they need to go on assignment for an undisclosed period of time and that they'll be back as soon as they can. As difficult as the departure may be, you both understand that it's their job to go and it's your job to wait.

Now imagine that they aren't allowed to contact you while they're away because of the danger it could impose on either you or them. Without knowing any of the details, your job is to simply wait and offer support from a distance until they return. While the initial goodbye could be so incredibly difficult, the waiting period without any communication could be both discouraging and devastating. Keep this scenario in mind as we continue on with the story of Moses and the Ten Commandments.

Moses went up the mountain out of obedience to God. The Israelites waited for him to return out of obedience to God as well. Remember, though we are given insight from Exodus 24:18 that Moses stayed on the mountain for forty days and forty nights, the Israelites were not privy to that information.

I think most of us would agree that waiting for Moses to return probably wasn't too difficult for the first few days. But as the days turned into weeks, and the weeks turned into a month, we can appreciate how difficult and frustrating their wait became. As Moses was getting instructions from the Lord, and the wait for his return lingered on, the Israelites got impatient. Would he ever come back?

Now be honest. Does anything good ever result when we get impatient? From my experience, the answer has always been a flat out "No!" Impatience doesn't result in anything good because impatience is not a fruit of the Spirit. Only patience can result in something that's good and godly. But true patience requires full dependence upon God through the power of the indwelling Holy Spirit. We can only demonstrate godly patience by keeping God in the picture. Apart from Him, we can do nothing.

As we move ahead in our story, we find that the people were growing very impatient and they were determined to take things into their own hands. Ugh! I've done that before, have you? When I've wanted results, and haven't seen them take place in the way or timeframe I've wanted, I've gotten impatient and have taken control. Big mistake ... HUGE! Nothing good comes from me taking charge over a situation in which God is already controlling.

So, what did the Israelites do in their hastiness? Exodus 32:1 says, "When the people saw that Moses was so long in coming down from the mountain, they gathered around Aaron and said, 'Come, make us gods who will go before us. As for this fellow Moses who brought us up out of Egypt, we don't know what has happened to him.'"

Isn't it interesting how they now referenced one of their leaders as "this fellow Moses?" It's as if he was just a stranger in their group who was causing them to be inconvenienced. Isn't it ironic that in their impatience, they seem to have lost respect for the one who was their direct communication link between themselves and the Almighty God? Also, they mentioned that they didn't know what had happened to Moses. Was it that they didn't know, or that they really didn't care? Hmmm, interesting thought.

So here they go, taking the situation into their own hands because they wouldn't stay committed to what they promised Moses earlier. They had promised that they would do everything the Lord had said and that they would obey. It's amazing how quick they were to back out on their promise once the wait time got extended past their personal expectations. Are we any different?

You see, the Israelites' response really represents us in this present day. When we get impatient, we start to get frustrated. We want answers and we want them now. As a result, we take control of situations in order to get results. We don't necessarily care what the results are anymore. We just have a need to feel like we're making progress. However, just because we're encouraged to be making progress, doesn't mean that we're moving in the right direction. The fact that we've taken control of a situation should be a warning sign to us that danger is ahead. There's danger because we've chosen to make a decision independent from God. Our job as Christians is to be fully dependent upon the Lord, even while we wait, no matter how long it takes. We must not rob God of His control over our lives. Depend on Him. Cling to Him while you wait.

So, what happened when the Israelites took control of their situation and decided they couldn't wait any longer for Moses to return from the mountain? In their impatience and impulsiveness, they asked Aaron to make gods who would go before them since they didn't know what happened to Moses. In response to their request, Aaron told them to take off the gold earrings from their wives, sons and daughters and bring them to him. Aaron took the items they handed him and made them into an idol cast in the shape of a calf. In simple terms, they made a god for themselves and began celebrating as they held a festival to the Lord. Their impatience caused them to deceive themselves into thinking they were worshiping the Lord when, in fact, God saw them as being a corrupt people who began worshiping a man-made golden calf.

Let this story be a caution to us, dear friends. We can become just like the Israelites if we're not careful. Our human need for control and answers is great in this fallen world, regardless of where we live. But God has a purpose for our wait. Our job is to simply trust and obey Him through it. It's natural that the longer we must endure our wait times, the more helpless we may become. But let me offer you some encouragement. Our helplessness truly is a gift from God if it directs our attention, communication and dependence upon the Lord. He is the provider of all good things. Our helpless state doesn't mean we are hopeless. It's quite the contrary. Our helpless state makes us hopeful when our eyes stay fixed on Him. God hears, He sees, He knows and He responds to His children. If we truly believe that, then we will wait with a hopeful heart. Joy and peace will flood our souls.

ABRAHAM AND ISAAC

Let's revisit the story of Abraham and Isaac from Genesis 22. If having a child in the later years of life wasn't enough for Abraham, God had a much bigger challenge in store for him. It would not necessarily be one he would welcome, but one that would test his devotion and obedience to the Lord. Not only would he bear a son with his wife Sarah, but he would be challenged to sacrifice his son as well.

Though we don't know how much time went by since Isaac was born, we know that it was some time later when God called out to Abraham with a task. God told him to take his only son, Isaac, to the region of Moriah. That location was about 50-60 miles from Beersheba and would require a traveling time of about three days. Once they got to their destination, Abraham was to sacrifice his son as a burnt offering on one of the mountains that the Lord would choose for them.

Can you even imagine the thoughts that must have been flooding his mind? Why would God be asking him to do such a thing to the only son he had waited to receive for so many years? Why would God test him in this way? Abraham didn't have all the answers, but he had faith in God, so he obeyed. Keep in mind that just because we choose obedience, it doesn't minimize or soften the task at hand. Obedience oftentimes comes with blood, sweat and tears.

Abraham's response was supernatural. He obeyed the difficult task assigned to him by God. Now stop and think about that for a moment. Can you even imagine what a weight that must have been for Abraham as he waited upon the Lord to sacrifice his son? Though his response to God was one of obedience, it doesn't mean he wasn't humanly overwhelmed and burdened by the task at hand. He loved the Lord and he loved his son. What a difficult situation to endure.

As the two of them walked along together, Isaac asked his father where the lamb was for the burnt offering. Abraham told him that God would provide the lamb. As he prepared his son on the altar to be sacrificed on top of the wood, and took the knife to slay his son, the angel of the Lord called out and said, "Do not lay a hand on the boy. Do not do anything to him. Now I know that you fear God, because you have not withheld from me your son, your only son" (Genesis 22:12).

That story overwhelms me every time I read it. I'm reminded that Abraham had such a tremendous fear and respect for God that he wouldn't let anyone or anything get in the way of his relationship with the Lord, not even his only beloved son. Wow! I'd like to say I have that same kind of faith each and every day, but I know my weaknesses. What a challenge this scenario would be for me. Being willing to sacrifice yourself would be difficult enough, but to lay your very own child down before the Lord would be excruciatingly painful. Remember, we have the opportunity to read the end of the story in Scripture to know that Abraham didn't have to go through the full act of killing his son, but Abraham had no idea what the end result would be until he kept taking one step at a time in faith as he obeyed God. What a testimony that Abraham longed to follow God's commands for his life more than he longed for the things of this world. He longed to obey God, despite the tremendous sacrifice.

I'm thankful that that's not a typical test required of us by God in this present day. However, God is still testing us through difficult situations. I'm hoping that none of you have had to lay a child down as a human sacrifice on an altar of wood, but it's possible that some of you have had to walk through a terminal illness with your child to the point that you've had to let them go. My heart aches for you. You've had to give them back to God and the pain was, and is, great. Others of you have had to walk through that same situation of a terminal illness, yet your child may have been spared of physical death.

It's impossible for us to grasp why God allows different outcomes for different people. Our job is to know that God loves us, despite the end results. Our job is to love and obey God through the tests and long for Him to pull us through the pain. When we prioritize God as our first love, we long for Him more than anything else. Our heart's desires begin to synchronize with God's desires. Our prayers transition from "My will be done" to "Thy will be done." Obeying God isn't always easy, but it's necessary as we walk with Him.

God requires different circumstances for different people. We don't get to pick and choose which commands we want to fulfill. God requires obedient hearts from His children. Regardless of how simple or sacrificial the task, God will walk us through every step of the way. All He expects is that we trust and obey.

DISCUSSION QUESTIONS:

1. Think back to the story of Moses when he went up the mountain and the Israelites had to wait for his return. Have you ever been in a situation where someone else was given a task or assignment, and you just had to wait for them to complete it without knowing when it would end? If so, what was the situation? Was it easy or hard for you to wait? Why?

   _____

   _____

   _____

   _____

2. In general, on a scale of 1-10 (1=low, 10=high), how patient would you say you are? _____

3. How quick are you to take control of situations when wait times get extended past your personal preferences? Share your thoughts.

   _____

   _____

   _____

   _____

4. If you are prone to being impatient, and you are quick to take control of situations instead of waiting upon the Lord, do you typically experience positive results? Explain.

   _____

   _____

   _____

   _____

5. Consider the story of Abraham when God asked him to sacrifice his son, Isaac. Though that is an extreme situation, has God ever asked you to sacrifice something out of obedience to Him that was humanly heartbreaking for you to endure? (For example, having to give up a job, a boyfriend, a friendship, a dream, etc.) Did you follow through? What did you learn from it? Share your thoughts.

_____

_____

_____

_____

12

PERSEVERE

I LOVE A PARTICULAR LESSON God taught me in His Word a couple of years ago. John 4 tells us about Jesus talking to a woman at the well. Verses 4-6 are most impactful to me. As the Scripture states, "Now he (Jesus) had to go through Samaria. So he came to a town in Samaria called Sychar, near the plot of ground Jacob had given to his son Joseph. Jacob's well was there, and Jesus, tired as he was from the journey, sat down by the well. It was about the sixth hour."

There is a specific phrase in verse 6, and a specific word within that phrase, that God has allowed to be of great encouragement to me. Read it below and see what jumps out at you:

"... and Jesus, tired as he was from the journey ..."

You may have just finished reading that phrase and are now thinking to yourself, "What's the big deal about those words? What does that have to do with anything, especially about waiting?" Allow me to share what God has spoken to my heart about them. It's been life-changing to me.

First of all, we are made aware that Jesus was tired. He had been on a long journey. He was traveling from Judea to Galilee which is about 70 miles. Jesus went through Samaria on His way to Galilee. The distance from Judea to Samaria is estimated to be a walking journey of 5-6 hours. That's quite a long hike by foot. This Bible passage confirms that we are not the only ones who have experience tiredness. Jesus experienced it as well. Don't you just love the fact that our Savior and Lord experienced human life, emotions and feelings just like we do now? Isn't it a relief to know that He can relate to us in every area of our lives? I'm so thankful that He knows we get tired. He knows what it feels like. He knows there are times when we need a break. He knows just how we feel in our tired state right now, dear friends. He sees, He knows and He cares about us every step of the way. That alone should be of great encouragement to us.

Second, we are told that Jesus was tired *from* the journey. It does not say Jesus was tired *of* the journey. Wow, that's been a tremendous eye-opener for me! There have been times in my Christian life when I've allowed my mind to think, "I'm sick of this Christian walk. I'm tired of it. I just can't go on like this anymore." Can you relate? Do you ever feel like being a Christian just isn't worth it anymore?

Ever since God revealed this passage to me, the Holy Spirit has given me a complete new outlook on my Christian life. Looking back, I've realized that I'm not sick and tired of my walk with God. I'm simply tired from the hardships, difficulties, trials and disappointments that come my way as I journey with God. And one of those difficulties can be waiting. It's exhausting. It seems unbearable at times. It can give me a false sense of hopelessness. But if God is allowing us to experience it, then it's necessary for our good and for God's glory. If it's necessary, then we must ask ourselves a question, "What will we do while we wait?" A more important question to ask is, "What did Jesus do while he waited?"

This brings us to the final point I wanted to share with you about this passage in John 4. We are told at the end of verse 6 that Jesus "sat down by the well" when He was tired from the journey. Though Christ was sitting by a physical well of water, we as Christians are to sit by the spiritual well of water to get a drink from the Living Water. In Jeremiah 2:13, God tells us that He Himself is the spring of Living Water.

John 1:1 reminds us that, "In the beginning was the Word, and the Word was with God, and the Word was God." The Word of God is our well that God intends for His children to thirst from. He desires that we long to take a drink from His Living Word to refresh our souls, give us strength, and encourage us to carry on the journey He has set before us. God reminds us that we will get tired *from* the journey. Specifically, this means that we will get tired from waiting for long periods of time in this life. But He also reminds us that we don't have to get tired *of* the journey or *of* the wait. Remember, He sees, He knows and He cares about every aspect of our lives.

When we get tired of something, we typically want out. We're either fed up with it or we're at our wits' end ready to give up. We've had it. Enough is enough. Can you relate? However, when we're tired from something, it simply means we're exhausted, weary or worn. We need to take a break but we're not giving up. We know we need to get refreshed so we can continue on and persevere with the task at hand.

Think of people who run marathons. They've got a 26.2–mile race before them. Though they've trained, the journey will still be strenuous on their bodies. After the first several miles, many of them may become physically, mentally or emotionally exhausted. They may want to give up, but their eyes are on the finish line and they've trained far too hard to quit now. As they run past the aid stations, they douse themselves with bottles of water and persevere. Though they're tired from the journey, they're not tired of the journey. This is what they've been called to do. They're determined to continue on. Their mission isn't over yet. Not until they cross the finish line.

Jesus was on a mission as well. He went from town to town healing, encouraging, baptizing and sharing the gospel with multitudes of people. He walked several hundreds, if not thousands, of miles as He ministered from one place to the next. His journey wasn't easy, but He was willing to persevere. He wouldn't give up because this was the reason He came. Yes, Jesus got tired from the journey. The walking and the ministering would've been mentally, physically and emotionally exhausting. But He didn't get tired of the spiritual journey. He knew why He was here. He knew the plans and purposes God had set before Him. He would stay on task until His Father brought Him home. He would persevere.

Isn't that so encouraging? Though Jesus got tired, He wasn't going to give up. He was determined to stay the course. Is that how it is for you and me? How about when the task we've been assigned is simply to wait for something? Will we persevere and wait as long as it takes without giving up?

Maybe you feel like you're experiencing a marathon of waiting right now. Maybe you've waited desperately over the past several months or years for answers, results or change. Will you wait as long as it takes? God is stretching and growing you while you wait. He is molding and making you into His likeness. Though you may get tired *from* the wait, may you keep persevering and not get tired *of* the wait. Go to the Living Well to be refreshed, dear friends. Only then will you be willing to wait as long as it takes.

PAUL AND SILAS PERSEVERED IN PRISON

Many times, we think of perseverance as being related to an action more than an attitude. But our attitudes are tied to our hearts. Our actions are an outpouring of our hearts into the lives of others. Perseverance is more about how we choose to *be* while we wait, more than what we choose to *do*.

A story that reflects the idea of a persevering attitude is found in Acts 16. This is the story of Paul and Silas. While the two were on their way to a place of prayer, they preached the gospel to those the Holy Spirit allowed to hear. As they traveled, they were met by a slave girl who earned a lot of money by fortune-telling. She followed Paul and Silas and shouted comments about them for many days. Paul became so troubled that he turned and commanded that the spirit leave her, and it did (vs 16-18).

The owners of the slave girl were angry when they realized their hope for making money through her fortune-telling was gone so they dragged Paul and Silas into the marketplace to face the authorities. The crowd attacked the men and the magistrates ordered Paul and Silas to be stripped and beaten.

In verse 23 we read that Paul and Silas were not just stripped and beaten, they were severely flogged. They were then put in prison where they were guarded carefully. The two men were put in the inner cell and their feet were fastened in the stocks. What was there for them to do now? They had no choice but to wait.

This is the part that amazes me the most. These men had been in ministry doing the work of the Lord. They were now waiting for their next assignment in jail. These men had been severely flogged. They were now waiting for healing. These men had been bound in a prison cell. They were now waiting to be rescued. And what did they do while they waited?

Verse 25 reveals their incredible response. At about midnight, Paul and Silas were praying and singing hymns to God. They worshiped the Lord while they waited. With their bodies badly beaten and battered, their attitudes rejoiced. They had no idea how long they'd have to wait in a prison cell before being released, but their attitudes of singing praises to the Lord, only moments after being beaten, demonstrated that they were willing to persevere. Though their circumstances were dismal, their hearts overflowed. Even a prison cell could not contain their joy. Oh, that we, too, would wait upon the Lord with an attitude of perseverance knowing that God is good all of the time. He is the reason we persevere.

MIGHTY WARRIORS

If you could select any professional title to attach to your name, what would you choose? Some may pick CEO, president, king, queen, professor, dean, admiral, sergeant, doctor, lawyer, CPA, Mr. or Mrs., etc. Titles tend to define us. They give people a sense of purpose, yet can come with a great sense of expectation, both by the individual themselves, as well as others.

While many of us go out in search for titles we desire for ourselves, it's unique to know that God gave titles to people in the Bible. They didn't have to obtain them on their own. They were actually assigned their titles by the Living God. One of the people whom God gave a significant title to was Gideon. His story is found in the book of Judges, Chapters 6–8.

Gideon was a simple farmer who was threshing wheat in a winepress. One day, the angel of the Lord appeared to him saying, "The LORD is with you, mighty warrior" (Judges 6:12). Now stop for a moment. Can you even imagine an angel of the Lord appearing to you in a winepress and defining you as a "mighty warrior" of God? Wow!

Though Gideon had been greeted with an amazing title by the angel, Gideon realized he was personally ill-equipped to fight the Midianites, even though God had chosen him for both the job and the title. God promised to be with him and give the Midianites into his hands. However, Gideon had every reason in the book why he shouldn't persevere. "The LORD has abandoned us" ... "My clan is the weakest" ... "I am the least in my family" ... etc. Excuses, excuses, excuses.

How many times do those responses reflect us? How many times do we make up excuses as to why we shouldn't, or won't, obey the Lord? Dear friends, it is our job to follow God. It's our responsibility. We are expected to persevere while we wait upon the Lord. This is our testimony of faith so that others may know in whom we believe.

Have you ever considered that you and I carry the same title of "mighty warrior" for the Lord if we have asked Jesus Christ to be our personal Lord and Savior? We are not mighty warriors because of the personal strength and power we possess. We are mighty warriors because of the mighty God we serve. He is our strength, He is our power and He is our shield. We need not be afraid to stand in the spiritual battles that come our way because God has already overcome them for us. We need to be strong in the Lord. It is His strength we possess and it is His power that will overcome all evil. We must simply persevere.

God's Word reminds us in 2 Timothy 1:7 that, "God did not give us a spirit of timidity, but a spirit of power, of love, and of self-discipline." He reminds us over and over again in Scripture to "fear not" for "He is with us."

As mighty warriors for Christ, we need to take a stand with confidence each and every day. We must be bold and unashamed of the gospel of Christ while we wait. We need to claim, and proclaim, the title God has given us as we claim the victory we have already won through Jesus Christ our Lord. Warriors don't quit. They persevere and experience a life of constant victory—victory in Jesus!

Taking this idea even one step further, I'm encouraged when I read Romans 8:37-39 because it reminds us that we are not just mighty warriors, dear friends. We are considered *more than conquerors* because nothing can separate us from the love of Christ. Not death nor life, neither angels nor demons, neither the present nor the future, nor any powers, neither height nor depth, nor anything else in all creation. Nothing can ever separate us from God. Hold fast to that promise and persevere while you wait.

GOD COMMANDS PERSEVERANCE

It's obvious we must persevere while we wait, but why? Did you realize that God actually commands perseverance from His chosen people? We are considered to be one of His chosen if we have accepted an eternal, saving relationship with Him through the shed blood of Jesus Christ on the cross.

Read the following Scriptures to help grasp how important the idea of perseverance is in a Christian's life, as well as the result of persevering:

- "You need to *persevere* so that when you have done the will of God, **you will receive what he has promised**" (Hebrews 10:36).

- "Blessed is the man who *perseveres* under trial, because when he has stood the test, **he will receive the crown of life** that God has promised to those who love him" (James 1:12).

- "*Perseverance* must finish its work so that **you may be mature and complete**, not lacking anything" (James 1:4).

Waiting is a trial. It's a test. It's a way of God teaching us to become fully dependent upon Him so we can be made mature and complete, lacking nothing. God is using our times of wait to renew us inwardly day by day. We persevere through the wait so we can die to self and become more like Christ. We persevere because we know this world is not our home. As believers in Christ, we are heaven-bound. We persevere because we are waiting for so much more than what this world has to offer.

DISCUSSION QUESTIONS:

1. Have you ever struggled in your Christian walk where you've been tired either *from* the journey or *of* the journey? Have you ever wanted your Christian journey to end? Share your thoughts.

   _____

   _____

   _____

   _____

2. How do you prepare yourself to respond in worship to God when you encounter difficulty?

   _____

   _____

   _____

   _____

3. Hopefully you haven't spent time in an actual prison cell, but have you ever experienced a time like Paul and Silas when they worshiped while they waited? Explain.

   _____

   _____

   _____

   _____

4. Are you, like Gideon, one who makes excuses as to why you won't, or shouldn't, obey God? Explain.

   _____

   _____

   _____

   _____

5. What comes to mind when you consider yourself having the title of *"mighty warrior?"*

_____

_____

_____

_____

6. What thoughts come to mind when you hear that you are *"more than conquerors?"*

_____

_____

_____

_____

13

WHAT ARE WE REALLY WAITING FOR?

IN THE FIRST CHAPTER OF this book, I provided a list of several different examples of things people wait for in life. Some of the things listed were exciting to wait for, and others were not. The list was not inclusive. What we can conclude, however, is that we've all had to wait for one thing or another. But in terms of what we've waited for, as well as the length of time we've had to wait for it, both of those can differ from person to person.

Review the list again from Chapter 1. In and of themselves, most of the items listed aren't necessarily bad things. They're realistic. However, take a few minutes to really evaluate the list. What thoughts or emotions flood your mind as you consider the various points? Be honest with yourself. God already knows your heart.

Now, take some time to consider the return of Christ. What thoughts or emotions flood you as you grasp that reality? Maybe this is the first time you've ever thought of that before. Don't rush it. Be honest as you ask yourself, "What are you truly waiting for?" Are you more eager for one or more of the things on the list, or for the return of Christ? Remember that the points on the list are only temporal and uncertain. The return of Christ is eternal and certain. Which one is most worth your time and effort as you wait?

Consider this thought. Whether we are aware of it or not, all believers are ultimately waiting for the exact same thing. Well, what is it? Each one of us is waiting for our Savior, the return of Jesus Christ. Psalm 27:14 says, "Wait for the LORD; be strong and take heart and wait for the LORD."

In Genesis, ever since sin entered the world, God's people have been waiting for the Lord's return. When David wrote Psalm 27, he was confident that he would see the land of the living. He was confident that he would experience heaven and meet Jesus face-to-face. Jesus Christ, the Savior of the world, had not even appeared yet. However, David kept an eternal focus and walked in step with God to know that the Lord was faithful and would carry out every one of His promises revealed in Scripture. David rested in the fact that the Lord was his Light and his Salvation so he need not fear while he waited for the Lord's will to be accomplished through him on earth (Psalm 27:1).

As Christians, our wait is the same as it was for Paul, David, Esther, Noah, Job, Habakkuk, Mary and all the other people in Scripture who trusted in God. For thousands of years, believers have been waiting for the Savior. But how long must we wait?

Habakkuk 2:3 says, "The revelation awaits an appointed time; it speaks of the end and will not prove false. Though it linger, wait for it; it will certainly come and not delay." This verse reminds us that God is not strapped or hindered by time the way we are. While we are constrained by time, God is free from its boundaries.

Many times, we think God allows periods of waiting in our lives to prolong, delay or frustrate us. But that's a lie we must caution ourselves not to believe. By getting impatient, we may start to doubt what is true. We must remember that God's Word is truth. Every word of the Bible is a fact and a certainty either of what has, or what is, to come. The problem lies in our anxiousness. Waiting goes against nearly every part of our fleshly being.

As we read further on in Habakkuk 2:4, we are reminded that, "The righteous will live by his faith." Our faith is in God and in the return of Jesus Christ, His Son. Our faith cannot rest in the concept of time. There are secret things of God that we'll never know. Rather than letting the hidden things of God frustrate or confuse us, we need to embrace the fact that the hidden things of God are what allow us to implement our faith and trust in Him. Faith and trust are needed when there are no answers. When life confuses us and all we can see are either unknowns or dead ends, that's when we have the opportunity to watch our faith at work. Rather than give up, it's our time to give in.

For many people, giving in means the same as giving up. Giving in simply means that we surrender our wants, needs and expectations to the Lord. We let God take control and give in to His plans and purposes. We rest in the fact that His thoughts and ways are always higher than ours. Ah, the joy and peace that comes by giving in and waiting for the plans of our Almighty God to unfold!

But how do we stay confident while we wait? We need to remind ourselves, and each other, of the promises God has left us in Scripture. Philippians 3:20 says, "But our citizenship is in heaven ..." Do you believe that, dear friends? When times get tough and we start to doubt the goodness of God, do we remind ourselves that this world is not our home? God has reminded us that we are foreigners and strangers to this world. We don't belong here. We need to be careful not to get too comfortable here or we won't want to leave. We're just passing through this life for a moment in time. We're on our way to an eternal paradise that God has reserved for each of His children who believe in the Name of His Son, Jesus.

As we read in Philippians 3:20-21, it not only tells us that our citizenship is in heaven, but because of that, "... we eagerly await a Savior from there, the Lord Jesus Christ who, by the power that enables him to bring everything under his control, will transform our lowly bodies so that they will be like his glorious body."

Think about the word *eager* for a minute. When we are eager for something, it means we have great anticipation. We long for it. We're excited for it. Keep in mind that we are to be eagerly awaiting a Savior, the Lord Jesus Christ. We are waiting for a Person. When life gets hard and I start to get discouraged, I find myself eager to be taken out of my difficulties and hardships rather than finding myself eager to truly see Jesus. It's a selfish eagerness I struggle with from time to time. I want my eagerness to be real. I want it to be genuine. I want to be so excited to see Jesus that I'm willing to minimize the frustrations of this world and stand watchful for His return with great anticipation. The waiting is bearable when I keep my eyes on the Person I'm going to meet, rather than on the situations I'm going to leave behind. Stay focused, stay watchful and stay eager for Jesus. He is coming, just as He said.

We are reminded by the minor prophets of how difficult it was as they prophesied among the unbelievers of their time. Day after day, they followed the Lord's calling upon their lives and kept warning the people to turn away from their idol worship and turn toward God. Their work was discouraging, repetitive and lacked results they were hoping for. Yet their faithfulness to God prevailed and their hearts remained steadfast in the Lord.

Among disappointment, the prophet Micah responded, "But as for me, I watch in hope for the LORD, I wait for God my Savior ..." (Micah 7:7). Among devastation, the prophet Habakkuk replied, "Yet I will rejoice in the LORD, I will be joyful in God my Savior." These are just a couple of examples for us to follow, dear friends. We can overcome the hardship and discouragement of waiting by changing our perspective. We can find peace and joy in the Lord. If we focus on the Person of Christ, there is hope. If we focus on the outcome of a situation, we will soon become hopeless.

1 John 3:1-2 says, "How great is the love the Father has lavished on us, that we should be called children of God! And that is what we are! The reason the world does not know us is that it did not know him. Dear friends, now we are children of God, and what we will be has not yet been made known. But we know that when he appears, we shall be like him, for we shall see him as he is."

The second verse states three words that give us a promise to motivate us while we wait—*when He appears*. This is both a statement and a promise telling us that it *will* happen. It's not a matter of "*if*" but "*when*."

Our humanness tends to be impatient, so rather than being motivated by the fact that Jesus *is* coming again, we tend to get hung up on *when* He's coming. That perspective is not motivating. We can't stay encouraged during our time of wait if we allow ourselves to doubt God's promises and perfect timing for all things.

We must continually praise the Lord on a daily basis saying, "Yes, Lord, You *are* coming again!" Look at the phrases below to see how a simple change in order of the second and third word can change a promise from belief to doubt:

"When I am" verses *"When am I?"*

The same three words are used in both phrases. The only difference is the order in which the words are placed. The first phrase proclaims a statement. The second one implies a question or doubt. The words in 1 John 3:2 declare a statement that should cause us to rejoice... *when He appears.* Yes, indeed, Christ will appear to us one day and that promise alone should be motivation enough to prepare our hearts to meet Him face-to-face. We shouldn't care so much about the time *when* He's coming, but rather focus on the fact that He *is* coming. Yes, He is coming soon! So, while we wait:

Hebrews 12:2

Let us fix our eyes on Jesus, the author and perfecter of our faith, who for the joy set before him endured the cross, scorning its shame, and sat down at the right hand of the throne of God.

Hebrews 10:23-25

Let us hold unswervingly to the hope we profess, for he who promised is faithful. And let us consider how we may spur one another on toward love and good deeds. Let us not give up meeting together, as some are in the habit of doing, but let us encourage one another—and all the more as you see the Day approaching.

1 Peter 1:13

Therefore, prepare your minds for action; be self-controlled; set your hope fully on the grace to be given you when Jesus Christ is revealed.

While we wait, it is our responsibility to stay focused. We must keep our eyes fixed on Jesus while encouraging others and remaining hopeful. The day of the Lord is approaching, dear friends. Be watchful and wait for it.

DISCUSSION QUESTIONS:

1. How often do you think about the return of Christ? What thoughts do you have?

   _____

   _____

   _____

   _____

2. How are you actively encouraging others toward love and good deeds as you wait for the return of Christ?

   _____

   _____

   _____

   _____

3. When you consider the return of Christ, does that make your earthly wait seem more bearable? Why or why not?

   _____

   _____

   _____

   _____

4. Philippians 3:20 reminds us that our citizenship is in heaven. We are mere aliens and strangers on this earth. What thoughts come to mind when you consider that we are *aliens and strangers?*

   _____

   _____

   _____

   _____

5. How easy is it for you to rest in the plans and purposes God has for your life? Do you struggle with control? Share your thoughts.

_____

_____

_____

_____

14

HOW LONG DO WE WAIT?

As humans, we're usually looking for specific times that pinpoint God to act on something. We either want it in the form of an hour and minute, as on a watch or clock, or we want a calendar date set aside so we can plan and prepare for a particular event to occur.

Society is quickly growing out of its desire to be surprised. Notice I used the words *growing out of* rather than *outgrowing*. It isn't that we've matured to the point of not needing to be surprised anymore. It's quite the contrary. I believe we're losing our sense of trust so we rely heavily upon the seen rather than the unseen. Unfortunately, due to terrorist attacks, school shootings, bomb threats, kidnappings, murders and abductions, the trust level within our country has been drastically reduced over a very short period of time. We now live in a world of predictions, alerts and warnings. We live in a technological world that likes to pinpoint dates so we can be "in the know." No one wants to be blindsided. We now fear the unknown more than ever before.

Though we are so eager to know specific dates and times, we must remember that God is not driven by time the same way we are. God's timetable has an eternal focus rather than a physical one.

I love an illustration of this that came up this past summer in one of my Sunday School classes. We were referencing the book of Revelation and came across the verse that says, "I am coming soon ..." (Revelation 3:11). All of us were curious as to what the word *soon* was implying.

A woman sitting nearby me reminded us that, *"With the Lord a day is like a thousand years, and a thousand years are like a day"* (2 Peter 3:8). She continued on to say that since we are in the 21st century, we have experienced approximately 2,000 years since the death of Jesus Christ. If a day is like a thousand years, then that means we've been waiting for only about 2 days to this point. Hmmm, interesting thought, huh? Even if Jesus returned in another 1,000 years that would merely be one more spiritual day, which would still be considered *soon* in God's eyes.

As I'm writing this, I'm reminded that God doesn't want us to bank all of our life's activities and decisions on a mere calendar or watch. No. He wants us to base our activities and decisions on our Lord, Jesus Christ. God doesn't want us to draw closer to our daily planners, He wants us to draw closer to our Deliverer. In order to do this, we must determine in our hearts to trust God wholeheartedly. We must trust that He knows the perfect time, dates and locations for all things and that He will reveal the specifics of those to us as He deems best. Though we may be eager for the specifics that are not revealed to us, we can rest assured that if it hasn't happened yet today, or in this exact moment in which we're living, then it still isn't the right time according to God.

We are reminded of the value God has placed on time as we reference Ecclesiastes 3:1-8 which says:

> *There is a time for everything, and a season for every activity under heaven: a time to be born and a time to die, a time to plant and a time to uproot, a time to kill and a time to heal, a time to tear down and a time to build, a time to weep and a time to laugh, a time to mourn and a time to dance, a time to scatter stones and a time to gather them, a time to embrace and a time to refrain, a time to search and a time to give up, a time to keep and a time to throw away, a time to tear and a time to mend, a time to be silent and a time to speak, a time to love and a time to hate, a time for war and a time for peace.*

Rather than asking, "What is the specific time for this God?" we simply need to respond by saying, "Thank you for knowing the specific time for this God." Can you hear the difference? The first question implies that we are demanding an answer from God, whereas the second response implies that we are accepting and trusting in the Lord who masters over our lives. There is anxiety associated with the first question. There is peace and rest that comes with the second.

Quite honestly, if we knew how long some of our wait times would be for different situations, many of us wouldn't stick them out as long as we think. For example, if you knew you were going to work for an irritating boss for the next 23 years who would promise you multiple promotions and never follow through with them, would you be apt to work for him or her for the whole 23 years, or do you think you'd start seeking new employment opportunities soon after taking the job? What if on your wedding day you were told that for the next 37 years your husband would not be the spiritual leader he committed to be as he said his vows to you? Would you be committed to staying married to him, or do you think you'd be looking for a way to keep your name off of the marriage license before even saying "I do?" What if you read on your child's birth certificate that he or she would gradually become rebellious in the years ahead and would eventually disown you as their parent by age 16? Would you be as eager to play with them each day and rock them to sleep every night? Or, what if you knew it would take 50 years of praying for a loved one before they finally made a commitment to accept Jesus Christ as their personal Lord and Savior? Would you be eager to pray every day for the next 50 years (18,250 days), or would you think to yourself, "Is this really worth it?"

You see, in our humanness we believe knowing timetables for everything is to our benefit. Yet, are you starting to understand how knowing the specifics of time can actually be to our detriment? As Jesus told the apostles in Acts 1:7, "It is not for you to know the times or dates the Father has set by his own authority."

Consider this ... could it be a blessing that God hasn't shared many specific dates and times with us in the Bible for things yet to come? Could this simply be so we will experience, through faith alone, the hope of assurance found in the book of Hebrews? As we read in Hebrews 11:1, "Now faith is being sure of what we hope for and certain of what we do not see." As we look at verse six of the same chapter, we find that, "... without faith it is impossible to please God, because anyone who comes to him must believe that he exists and that he rewards those who earnestly *seek him*" (emphasis added). Our job is to seek and desire God more than we seek and desire a specific date or time for something. The Creator of time is more important than the creation of time itself.

Speaking of seeking a specific date and time, allow me to share a situation that I recently found myself in to help illustrate this point. Personally, I found it rather humorous.

It was a week before my sister's birthday so I went to the post office to mail her a gift. Since she lives several states away, and postage is typically based upon the weight of a package and the distance it needs to travel, I've learned that the most economical way for me to mail things to her is via Priority Mail. The flat rate shipping boxes typically work great for me. As I paid for my postage, the clerk printed out my receipt. Upon handing it to me, she said, *"Now your receipt is confirming a delivery date of Thursday, which is three days from now. However, we don't guarantee that date. In reality, it may take between seven to ten business days for it to be delivered."* WHAT?!?! I just paid for a confirmed delivery date of three days and mailed the package a whole week in advance to guarantee an early arrival date. Yet now I'm being told that it may take two to three times longer for her to receive the package I was sending?! How does that work? That made absolutely no sense to me at all. However, as I typically do, I took the receipt, smiled politely at the clerk and thanked her for her help.

As I walked to my car a bit frustrated, God reminded me of something. Even when we pay money to speed up time and expedite delivery dates, there's simply no guarantee that the delivery will take place within that designated period of time. In fact, there are instances when a package may not get delivered at all due to it getting lost, stolen or possibly sent to the wrong address altogether. These are reasons why some people opt to purchase insurance for their mailed packages. The insurance guarantees that if their package doesn't get to its destination, the customer can at least be reimbursed for the estimated cost of the items that were shipped.

Applying this concept to our spiritual lives, we need to remember that we, too, as children of God, are waiting for a special delivery. That special delivery is the return of Jesus Christ when He comes to gather His children and take us to heaven to live with Him forever and ever. The Bible clearly states multiple times in the book of Revelation that Jesus *is* coming. He is coming *soon*. However, it also reminds us that no one, not even the angels, know the day or hour when the Son of Man will come (Matthew 24:36-37). This information belongs to God alone. We need not get discouraged over the unknown date or time of our Savior's return. We simply need to rest upon the promise of the One who promised it. We need to trust in *Who* is coming rather than *when* He's coming. Our faith is stretched and strengthened by the things we cannot see.

IN THE COURSE OF TIME

Recently I've been reading through the book of First Chronicles. As I read through Chapters 18 and 19, God opened my eyes to the first five words that begin both chapters. They start with the following phrase, "In the course of time ..." In both instances, I found myself asking God, "What time frame are you talking about?" "How much time has passed by?" "How long did it really take?"

As I did a little more research, I found that this same phrase is referenced a total of 12 times in the NIV (New International Version) Bible to begin other sentences in the Old Testament. How remarkable that God doesn't need to reveal His specific timetable to us in all things. This has caused me to realize that though God's specific timing for everything is perfect and necessary for our good and His glory, the length of time that we wait for things should not bring us to the point of crisis. Waiting is important and necessary if we are waiting upon the Lord to work in us so we will desire and act according to His pleasure (Philippians 2:13). We tend to view our periods of waiting as a *curse* of time while God views them as a *course* of time. Oh God, change our perspective and perception to be more like Yours.

Undeclared time frames make many people uneasy. You see, our human minds have a hard time accepting the idea of time periods being mentioned without actual start and end dates being specified. We're troubled when we don't know how long something lasted in the past, or how long something will take in the future. We're prone to the known things in life because that's what helps our minds determine if something is really worth the wait or not. Time helps us put a value on things. Knowing the exact time frame of activities and circumstances helps us determine if the time frame is acceptable to us or not.

I usually dread it when I need to call a company's customer service department for a question or concern. Here's why … I'm usually put on hold for an undisclosed period of time, I have to listen to the same circle of music being played over and over in my ear while I wait, I hear their electronic voice repeat over and over of how sorry they are that I am still waiting, the voice reconfirms that someone should be with me shortly, and after all that waiting, my call sometimes is dropped or ended for one reason or another meaning that the waiting process will have to start all over again if I have any chance of getting my issue resolved. Has that ever happened to you? Ugh!

On the flip side, I've had some positive experiences when making customer service calls. One of my favorite things now is when I call a company that can give me an estimated waiting time, or they might let me know how many callers are ahead of me. That, in itself, can provide such a sense of relief. Even when I hear that my wait time is expected to be 25 minutes, or I'm told that I'm the seventh caller in line, I feel a weight lifted because I haven't been left stranded with the unknown. I know where I stand even if I don't like it. I'm able to endure a longer wait period simply because the company cared enough to let me in on their process. When I don't know how long my wait time may be, I get agitated much quicker. Each passing moment feels like forever. My inquiring mind wants to know where I stand, and it wants to know *now*. However, isn't it interesting how many times we're not given the specifics as to how long we must wait for the majority of things in life?

God is not hindered by time the way we are. We're reminded of that by simply acknowledging that God is the Alpha and Omega. He is the beginning and the end. God always was and He always will be (Revelation 1:8). There was never a beginning date for God and there will never be an ending date for Him. He always was, always is and always will be God. It's unfathomable for us to grasp the concept of infinity with God. But He never intended for our human minds to grasp it. He simply wants us to accept it and trust it. Along with His existence, the infinity of God is also mentioned in Scripture as it refers to His love. We are told in Ephesians 3:17-19 that God's love for us is wide, long, high and deep. Verse 19 tells us that we are, "To know that this (His) love surpasses knowledge." Again, we are not to understand His unending and unfailing love to the full. We are simply expected to accept the greatness and fullness of His love. Though God is too mighty for our minds to grasp, He will never be too mighty for our hearts to accept. Unfathomable, incomprehensible, yet acceptable.

There are many references in Scripture indicating various time periods where people had to wait upon the Lord in order to experience desired or promised outcomes. It's important for us to remember that most of the individuals listed in the following chart were ordinary human beings like us. They didn't have special super powers in the area of waiting. They had emotions and feelings—just like us. They had to deal with the unknowns and uncertainties of life—just like us. And ultimately, they had to put their trust in God alone—just like us. God requires all of His children to have faith in Him. There are no exceptions.

It's also important for us to remember that we have the privilege of reading about the start and end dates to the waiting periods for each of the biblical individuals being referenced. While that's a comfort to us, keep in mind that these people didn't necessarily know how long they'd have to wait upon the Lord for their revealed outcome. They weren't able to wait because their circumstances were easier than ours, or because they predetermined that their wait times were acceptable in their minds. No. They simply waited based upon their faith in God. They knew that their faith in God needed to far surpass their faith in time. Though this is an easy concept to talk about, it's quite another to live out.

Take a look at the following list of individuals referenced from Bible times and imagine what it was like for each of them to endure the circumstances that God allowed them to endure for differing lengths of time. Some were short and some were long. They dealt with situations tied to health, rebellion, change of position/status, fearful situations, etc. Even though we might not be able to comprehend their exact experience, we all can relate to the fact that a day can seem like a year when we wait.

Biblical Person	Life Situation / Circumstance	Waiting Period	Scripture
Jonah	Sat in the belly of a big fish	3 days and 3 nights	Jonah 1:17
Paul	Warned the Ephesian Elders with tears of what was to come	3 years	Acts 20:31
Aeneas	Bedridden paralytic	8 years	Acts 9:33
Woman	Subjected to bleeding	12 years	Mark 5:25 Luke 8:43
Woman	Crippled/bound by a spirit	18 long years	Luke 13:11
David	Waited from the time he was anointed to be king of Israel until he actually reigned as King	20 years	1 Samuel 16:13 2 Samuel 5:3-5
Abraham	Waited to become the father of many nations	25 years	Genesis 12:1-4 Genesis 17:1-14 Romans 4:16-20
Jesus	Waited to begin His ministry	30 years	Luke 3:23
Unnamed Man	Disabled (blind, lame, and/or paralyzed)	38 years	John 5:5
Israelites	Ate manna and wandered in the desert	40 years	Exodus 16:35

God	Endured rebellious conduct of the Israelites	40 years	Acts 13:18 Acts 7:30 Hebrews 3:9
Herod the Great	Remodeled the temple of the Lord	46 years	John 2:20
Abraham / Sarah	Desired to have a son	100 years / 90 years	Romans 4:19
Noah	Built an ark in the desert among wicked people	120 years	Genesis 6:3

Looking at this list, we see evidence that there was an end to each of their waiting periods. But we must keep in mind that most of those individuals didn't know when the end of their wait times would come— or if they'd come at all. They didn't know how their situations or struggles would pan out. They were no different than we are now. They had to trust in the Lord just like we do. They are our examples of what it means to have faith in God while we wait, regardless of the outcome.

Isaiah 49:8 says, "In the time of my favor I will answer you, and in the day of salvation I will help you ..." How incredible to think that when God chooses to answer us, it is truly in the time of His favor. We are constantly saying, "Not my will but Thy will be done, O Lord," however, do we really mean this? This verse has given me a completely different perspective regarding waiting. I am so much more willing to wait for lengthy periods of time now that I know that His answer will result in His favor. It's having a godly perspective that keeps us encouraged while we wait. A human perspective drags us down. We can consider waiting to be a privilege if we understand that His answer demonstrates His favor upon us. Yes, waiting upon the Lord is always worth the wait.

If you're convinced that you can't wait long enough, you're mistaken. Ask God to renew your mind. You *can* wait upon the Lord based on what God tells us in Lamentations 3:22-24:

> *Because of the LORD's great love we are not consumed, for*
> *his compassions never fail. They are new every morning;*

great is your faithfulness. I say to myself, "The LORD is my portion; therefore I will wait for him."

God is our provider. He has given us everything we need to get through every single day and every single waiting period that comes our way. Because of God's love, God's compassion and God's faithfulness, we can wait. Because God's grace is sufficient for us, we can wait. Because God's mercies are new every morning, we can wait. Renew our minds, dear Lord, and remind us that we can wait.

DISCUSSION QUESTIONS:

1. How much are you tied to calendars and/or watches to know when specific events will take place? Explain.

    _____

    _____

    _____

    _____

2. Are you glad God hasn't revealed specific dates and times to you regarding certain events or outcomes in your life, or do you wish He revealed all dates and times to you? Share your thoughts.

    _____

    _____

    _____

    _____

3. What's the longest you've had to wait for something? If you would've known how long you had to wait for that, do you believe you truly would've stuck out the wait for the entire time, or do you think you would've given up on the wait much earlier? Why?

    _____

    _____

    _____

    _____

4. As Christians, we know it's right to have a mentality that says, *"Not my will, but Thy will be done."* Do you truly believe you own those words in your heart so you actually live them out rather than just recite them? Explain.

    _____

    _____

    _____

    _____

5. Look at the chart referenced a few pages back in this chapter that includes the various biblical names, situations and their waiting periods. What stands out to you when you review that list?

_____

_____

_____

_____

15

FINAL THOUGHTS

I FIND IT INTERESTING THAT, as I've written this book from cover to cover over the past several years, God has allowed me to experience long periods of waiting that haven't been easy. To be completely honest, the past few years have been painfully difficult to endure. Though I enjoy writing, the amount of energy I have inside me gets bottled up and I want to shout out, *"What's my purpose in doing this, God? What plans do you have for me? Where will you use me? Will I ever have a sense of significance, worth or value in this life? It's lonely sitting here at home being obedient to you in the quiet. What are you doing, God? I feel like I'm wasting my time as I wait for Your direction in my life!"*

Can you relate? Do you know what that's like? The process of our waiting periods can be long, hard, and at times, extremely lonely. Have you been there? Maybe you're experiencing that type of season right now. Know that I understand, dear friends. But more importantly, God understands. Rest assured that the pain of your wait may be great, but our God is greater!

While I've watched and waited for God's direction over the years, I've seen glimpses of good and godly opportunities where I've longed to be involved. Yes, God has opened doors to several different opportunities just enough so I could see a potential plan, purpose and direction for my life. I've responded to God by saying "Yes" to each of those exciting prospects, telling Him that I've been both willing and able to pursue any one of the opportunities He's let me see at a glance. Unfortunately for me, as soon as

I've said "Yes Lord, I'm ready and willing," it has seemed as if God has put a wedge in the door so it can't open wide enough for me to walk through.

The first several times this happened, it was discouraging and frustrating, almost maddening at times. But the more it has happened, the more I see that God is testing my heart as I wait upon Him. He's showing me where I take control and create expectations that He never intended for me in the first place. He's teaching me that He may allow me to see *good* opportunities, but He will reserve only the *best* ones for me to pursue because He will always protect me. He will give me what I need when the timing and situation is right. I don't need to like it or understand it. I simply need to live it out and trust His best for my life.

God's also teaching me to have a willing heart that continues to be submissive to Him through the whole process of the wait. It's natural for us to be comfortable waiting upon the Lord in the beginning or near the end of our wait. The real challenge comes when we must live it out in the middle. Keep in mind that, "The ways of the LORD are right; the righteous walk in them, but the rebellious stumble in them" (Hosea 14:9). Keep walking through your wait, dear friends. Don't rush it or prolong it. Be watchful and prepare to move when God speaks. Embrace it and be willing to learn from it. God is teaching and growing you through it.

After years of feeling like I've been in a season of drought, I've learned some valuable lessons along the way. As potential opportunities have come about, I've learned to receive those from God with a willing "Yes." Then I quickly remind myself to surrender those opportunities right back to Him so He can do with them as He pleases.

Be willing to release the control that God already has in His grip. Don't fight Him for it. It was never meant to be a tug-of-war. God's teaching me what it really means to live out the phrase, "Not my will, but Thy will be done." I'm slowly learning that there is joy both in *receiving* from God, and in *releasing* to God. May we learn not to cling so tightly to the gifts and opportunities granted to us from the Lord. They are His, not ours. May we simply keep learning to cling to God, and hold loosely to everything else.

Be encouraged, dear friends, to enjoy the freedom God has always intended for us while we wait upon the Lord. We must wait upon Him until we learn what He will do for us. He is faithful and He will do it. He is worth the wait!

Discussion Questions:

1. Has your season of wait become painful? If so, what can you do to stay encouraged and hopeful?

    _____

    _____

    _____

    _____

2. Is it easier for you to *receive* from God or *release* to God? Share your thoughts.

    _____

    _____

    _____

    _____

3. What's one practical lesson you've learned about waiting that you can apply to your life so you become better equipped at waiting upon the Lord?

    _____

    _____

    _____

    _____

References

Chapter 1

What's Your Question? (n.d.). Retrieved from http://www.reference.com/

Bizarre and Random Facts. (n.d.). Retrieved from http://www.thefactsite.com/

Chapter 3

Miller, P. E. (2017). *A Praying Life: Connecting with God in a Distracting World.* Colorado Springs, CO: NavPress.

Chapter 6

M. (2017, February 17). MercyMe—"Even If" (Official Lyric Video). Retrieved from https://www.youtube.com/watch?v=B6fA35Ved-Y

Bennett, A. (1975). *The Valley of Vision: A Collection of Puritan Prayers and Devotions.* Edinburgh: Banner of Truth Trust.

Chapter 8

Heald, C. (2014). *Becoming a Woman Whose God is Enough.* Colorado Springs: NavPress.

Furtick, S. (2017, June 15). "Passing Your Test." Retrieved from https://www.youtube.com/watch?v=EX67U2p2YrA

Chapter 9

'Extraordinary' Minus God Equals Failure—Devotional | *Walk in the Word*, James MacDonald Bible Teaching. (n.d.). Retrieved from https://www.jamesmacdonald.com/teaching/devotionals/2005-11-14/

Greene, V. (n.d.). Dance in the rain by Vivian Greene. Retrieved from https://simplereminders.com/20151106221334.html

Chapter 10

Qubein, N. R. (2014). *Uncommon Sense*. Naperville, IL: Simple Truths.

ABOUT THE AUTHOR

 Amy has a fervent heart for the Lord and is a woman of integrity. She is a trusted source of spiritual nourishment and encouragement for those desiring to grow deeper in their relationship with God. Amy has shared God's Word to women of all ages for over 20 years. She's taught through many venues including Bible Studies, Sunday School classes, retreats, seminars, conferences and workshops. Amy is purposeful in the way she shares Scripture and incorporates it in a way that impacts listeners to not only hear God's Word but also apply it to their lives. Amy is gracious, compassionate and inspirational as she joyfully serves the Lord. She is an author, speaker, teacher and student of God's Word.

Amy is also passionate about helping individuals develop their personal and professional leadership skills. She is a trained facilitator for Leader to Leader Group Coaching and helps people grow in areas such as personal strengths and values, team building, shared visions, healthy communication, conflict resolution, and adapting to change.

You are invited to connect with Amy through her website at:
www.amyrauman.com